Rip it up

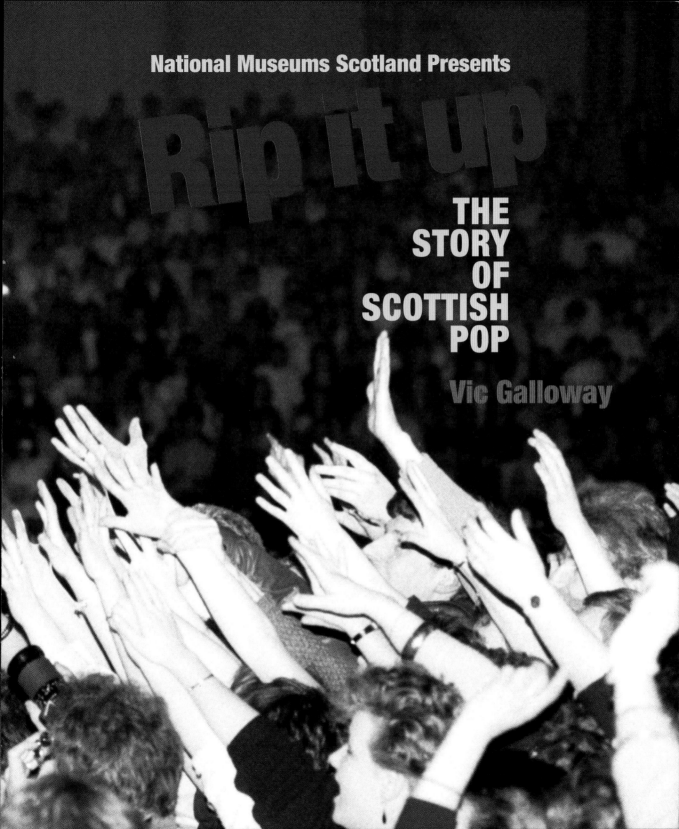

National Museums Scotland Presents

Rip it up

THE STORY OF SCOTTISH POP

Vic Galloway

RIP IT UP
The Story of Scottish Pop

Exhibition at
National Museum of Scotland
Chambers Street
Edinburgh EH1 1JF

www.nms.ac.uk

22 June to 25 November 2018

_____

National Museums Scotland
would like to thank
Baillie Gifford Investment Managers
for their generous sponsorship of this exhibition.

First published in 2018 by
NMS Enterprises Limited – Publishing
a division of NMS Enterprises Limited
National Museums Scotland
Chambers Street, Edinburgh EH1 1JF

www.nms.ac.uk

ISBN 978 1 910682 15 9

British Library Cataloguing-in-Publication Data
A catalogue record for this book is available on request from the British Library.

The publisher has made every effort to clear all copyright permissions, but where this has not been possible and amendments are required, the publisher will be pleased to make any necessary arrangements at the earliest opportunity.

Printed and bound in Latvia by PNB Printers.
Design of cover/title spreads by Mark Blackadder; based on concept by NMS Exhibitions and Design.
NMS photography by Photographic Studio, NMS Collections Services.

For a full listing of NMS Enterprises Limited – Publishing titles and related merchandise:

www.nms.ac.uk/books

Contents

Chapters

Introduction

Vic Galloway

Pop music could arguably lay claim to being the greatest, most influential global art form of the twentieth century and beyond. It has certainly helped to shape all other major cultural forms such as film, fashion, literature, design and visual art – not to mention international politics, social mobility and the fight for civil rights. Over seven decades, Scotland and its artists have played a major role in the development and success of pop music, from its very genesis to the countless genres today. Just don't mention *Donald Where's Yer Troosers!*

It was Edwyn Collins who wanted to rip it all up and start again on his seminal 1983 hit single with Orange Juice, referencing on multiple levels some elusive crush, a homage to his own musical influences and some kind of off-the-cuff manifesto for the future. Co-opting his song title *Rip It Up* for this book on the history of Scottish popular music seems wholly appropriate somehow. Scotland may seem like an improbable place for pop culture to have blossomed, and yet against all the odds it has.

Plucky, determined, defiant, daring and stubborn, Scotland is a country that will not be kept down. Whether through some kind of sense of injustice or an overriding ambition to accomplish the impossible, this small, aspirational country of approximately five and a half million people is a classic case of triumph over adversity. This is a place where music and song are the lifeblood of the community and where artistic expression is a national passion.

Scotland has always been both outsider and central player. Over hundreds of years it has simultaneously succeeded within a secure, stable union of nations and retained a spirit of independence and awareness of its own national identity. Out on the furthest reaches of north-western Europe, it is a unique combination of harsh weather, natural beauty, black humour, work ethic, secular enlightenment, religious sectarianism, educational excellence, generational poverty, working-class pride, spoils of empire and a blend of ancient ethnicities. It is a complex country full of contradictions, yet among the things that unify its people are its art, poetry, song-writing and storytelling.

From the experts and fans, insiders and onlookers, this book charts the sights, sounds and stories of the artists who have made the music and the crowds who have enjoyed the visceral thrill of homegrown pop throughout the years. It also discusses such questions as: What defines Scottish pop? How much impact has it had on the rest of the world? Who are its greatest successes? And which artists have led the way?

The roots of Scottish pop are examined, and the effect of post-war affluence in the 1950s, the baby-boomer generation and the arrival of the teenager. As Scotland reacted to Black American rhythm'n'blues and rock'n'roll, Lonnie Donegan became the poster-boy and hitmaker for a new, everyman form of music known as 'skiffle', influencing none other than The Beatles. When the beat boom arrived in the 1960s, Lulu became the household name, The Poets briefly gave The Rolling Stones a run for their money, Jack Bruce rocked the world in Cream and The Incredible String Band blended psychedelia and folk music to inimitable effect.

During the 1970s it was the tartan-clad Bay City Rollers who topped the charts in the United Kingdom, Gerry Rafferty conquered America and The Sensational Alex Harvey Band stirred up the ongoing counter-culture as social, economic and political times got harder. With the arrival of punk and new wave, Scotland was a pioneer once again, spawning the uncompromising Edinburgh agitators the Fire Engines and Josef K, chart-bound heroes like The Rezillos and Altered Images, and the post-punk indie template of Fast Product and Postcard Records.

By the 1980s Scottish pop had come of age with global success and notoriety. As money sloshed around the economy, a new optimism and materialism appeared in fashion and music as it fractured into separate parts. There was 'The Big Music' of Simple Minds and Big Country, the 'blue-eyed soul' of Wet Wet Wet and Hue & Cry, the roughshod jangle of 'C86' indie bands The Pastels and The Jesus and Mary Chain, the back-to-basics attitude of troubadours The Proclaimers, the dawn of rave culture, and the rise of Prince collaborator and bonafide pop star Sheena Easton.

In the 1990s grunge trailblazers Nirvana proclaimed their love for Bellshill's Teenage Fanclub and covered songs by The Vaselines. Post-recession, as relative political and financial stability reigned, Britpop arrived and Scotland's scene flourished with mainstream phenomena like Primal Scream, Travis, and Garbage with Shirley Manson. Another wave of independent labels emerged from Glasgow's thriving underground, seeing Mogwai, Arab Strap and Belle & Sebastian break into radio and the hearts and minds of fans. Scotland's music continued to blaze a trail across the world.

At the millennium, with Devolution and the establishment of Scotland's own Parliament, two decades of the most successful popular music began and continues today, despite the global financial crash of 2008. From guitar bands to singer-songwriters to world-beating electronic producers, Scotland punches above its weight and has shown how local can become global in the internet age. Calvin Harris is the most successful male solo artist in the States since Michael Jackson, KT Tunstall has sold millions of albums and had songs featured in Hollywood film soundtracks, while Franz Ferdinand reinvented indie rock and conquered festival stages across the world. Renowned songwriters Paolo Nutini, Amy Macdonald, and the edgier grassroots folk-influenced artists like King Creosote, have all achieved acclaim. Scotland can also lay claim to two of the UK's biggest rock bands, Biffy Clyro and Twin Atlantic, while Chvrches is regarded as a genuine pop sensation. Hip hop also flourishes, with the producer Hudson Mohawke and the arrival of explosive, multi-ethnic trio Young Fathers.

In writing this book I have tried to include as many artists as I could, but it was impossible to feature every musician associated with Scottish pop that has ever graced a stage or recording studio from the 1950s until today. Instead, I hope to showcase some of the players, the success stories and the wide-eyed innovators. As a musician, music fan, broadcaster and journalist, I am honoured to help document this exciting, exhilarating story. All the opinions that you see in this book are my own – all I ask is that you strap yourself in, hang on to yer troosers and enjoy the ride!

Opposite: Dancing at The Locarno, Glasgow, 1960

Acknowledgements and thanks

Individuals

M K Galloway, R D Galloway, Alan Galloway, Stephen Allen, Kevin Pocklington, Lindsay Gillies, Sharon Mair, Nicola Meighan, M I Wilson

Publications

Haslam, Dave 2015: *Life after Dark: A History of British Nightclubs and Music Venues* (Simon & Schuster).

Galloway, Vic 2013: *Songs in the Key of Fife* (Polygon, imprint of Birlinn Ltd).

Hogg, Brian 1993: *The History of Scottish Rock and Pop: All that ever Mattered* (Guinness).

Kielty, Martin 2006: *Big Noise: The Sound of Scotland* (Black & White Publishing).

Molleson, Kate 2015: *Dear Green Sounds: Glasgow's Music through Time and Buildings* (Gresham Publishing Company).

Papadopoulus, Harry (Ken McCluskey, ed) 2013: *What Presence! – The Rock Photography of Harry Papadopoulos* (Polygon, imprint of Birlinn Ltd) (e-book, Polygon).

Strong, Martin C 2002 – *The Great Scots Musicography: The Complete Guide to Scotland's Music makers* (Mercat Press).

Wilkie, Jim 1991: *Blue Suede Brogans: Scenes from the Secret Life of Scottish Rock Music* (Mainstream Publishing).

Websites

https://www.wikipedia.org/
https://www.youtube.com/
https://www.discogs.com/
https://www.allmusic.com/
www.7tt77.co.uk
www.rockingscots.co.uk
https://scotbeat.wordpress.com
www.nnevents.scot
http://www.edinburghgigarchive.com

Radio documentaries

BBC Radio Scotland: 'Beat Stalking'.
BBC Radio Scotland: 'The Barrowlands'.
BBC Radio Scotland: 'Songs from the Kingdom'.
BBC Radio Scotland: 'The Story of Scottish Pop'.

TV and film documentaries

BBC Scotland 2008: 'Caledonia Dreamin'.
McPhee, Grant (director): 'Big Gold Dream: The Sound of Young Scotland 1977–1985' (Digital Onset Films, On-Set Digital and Tartan Features).

About the Author

Vic Galloway is a Scottish broadcaster, journalist, musician and author. He has presented for BBC Radio 1 and currently champions new music on BBC Radio Scotland every week and regularly on BBC 6 Music and the BBC World Service.

Note about images

Please note that the images used in this book are historical documentations of their period.

Dedication

This book is dedicated
to Stewart Cruickshank and to Scott Hutchison
– constant sources of music, art, inspiration, love and laughter –
Rest in Peace xxx

Chapter one

That's the way it's got to be

'A wop bop a loo bop, a lop bam boom!' screamed Little Richard beneath a lacquered pompadour and thick make-up, hammering at a piano as if possessed by the devil. Primal, guttural exclamations like these rang out across the airwaves and jukeboxes of the late 1950s, sparking a seismic change as the impending '60s 'Youthquake' erupted. The teenager was well and truly born and life would never be the same.

In a remote northwestern corner of Europe it had exactly the same effect – particularly in the two main population epicentres of Edinburgh and Glasgow. Soon Dundee, Perth, Aberdeen, Stirling, Inverness, even Elgin, would follow suit. Rock'n'roll and everything in its wake had arrived and Scotland would feel its full force.

As post-war austerity slowly began to ease, young people had more spare time and loose change in their pockets. The baby boom went bang – attitudes, fashions, tastes and times were a-changing. The fusing of Black American rhythm'n'blues and gospel with country and western and hillbilly folk influences created a new kind of American music that quickly spread across the States into Europe and beyond. However, it has to be remembered that racism and segregation were commonplace in parts of the USA at that time and it was not until performers such as Elvis Presley, Jerry Lee Lewis and Johnny Cash got involved in this new style of music that wider audiences would finally get on board.

It was the film 'Blackboard Jungle' that truly spread the be-quiffed rock'n'roll gospel far and wide across the United Kingdom, with Bill Haley and the Comets' single *Rock Around The Clock* going straight to number one in 1955. Despite Haley being considerably older and paunchier than his audience, and the song itself sounding a little tame in comparison to others, the effect of the movie, the single and live UK concert appearances ignited a fuse and set the touchpaper. The new-found Teddy Boy look and 'rebel without a cause' stance provoked signs in ballrooms stating 'No Edwardian Dress' in an attempt to hold wild youth at bay. It did no good of course. Yes there was occasional violence, but there was also enormous excitement and in time these venues would open their doors to the so-called 'devil's music'.

Pages XII–1: Exterior of the Locarno
dance hall, Glasgow, at night, *c*.1960s

That's not to say Scotland was immediately open to everything London was. Away from the cultural fulcrum of the time, life was far more conservative. The Church was all-powerful and central to daily life, and up to this point in the '50s live entertainment had been somewhat different too. While accordionist Jimmy Shand was having family-friendly hits with his Scottish country-dance band, Harry Lauder-style crooners were filling the clubs. The big bands packed out dance halls to the sound of swing, while occasional New Orleans-style jazz bands were just as popular.

Around forty active dance halls and ballrooms kept their doors open after the Second World War, creating a network of nightspots throughout the country. But this new music revolution demanded its own hang-outs, and pubs, clubs and coffee-shops were soon being booked by emerging local promoters hoping to make a fast buck from the newfangled craze.

At first there were few British bands familiar with this emerging music as the records would arrive initially as import vinyl from America. Quickest of the old-guard to adapt were the 'Dixieland' and modern jazz bands – the smaller, tighter units

Teddy boy in a nostalgia shop, 1978

usually consisting of guitar, bass, drums, possibly keyboards and a horn or two. As the media hailed the arrival of this rock'n'roll and audience tastes began to adapt, smaller bands incorporated the new sound into their repertoire, mixing it with jazz standards, New Orleans shuffle, jump blues and rhythm'n'blues. Glasgow-based Ricky Barnes All Stars were one of the first bands in Scotland, and in the UK, to embrace this rock'n'roll. Alongside other trailblazers such as the Bobby Patrick Big Six and Clyde Valley Stompers, they played packed shows across the country and appeared on television. Without a record deal, however, the All Stars did not progress in the public eye, but they were true pioneers, fuelling the musicians around them with passion and knowledge for the embryonic sounds.

Meanwhile a certain Anthony Donegan, born in Glasgow to Irish parents, was about to become a name on the lips of every teen music fan. Moving to East London at ten years old, he immersed himself in folk music and learned the banjo and guitar, harbouring musical ambitions as he grew older. Lifting his famous moniker 'Lonnie' from American singer Lonnie Johnson, whom he once supported at the London Festival Hall, his first real break came from songs performed in 1954 with the Chris

Jimmy Shand and his Band, May 1956

Barber Jazz Band – *John Henry* and *Rock Island Line*. Soon he went solo with a repertoire of country-blues, railroad songs and covers of work by the American folk and blues musician Lead Belly. This stripping back to the rawest forms of folk and rock'n'-roll was named 'skiffle', which took off in a big way. Such songs were easy to thrash away at on an acoustic guitar and Donegan became the poster-boy for the new movement. Every school band and most professionals on the club circuit incorporated these songs and ramshackle style. Accessible and utterly do-it-yourself, all you required was a tea-chest bass, steel-string guitar and a washboard for percussion. Skiffle became a phenomenon overnight.

Donegan may have been London-based, but he was most definitely rooted in Scottish and Irish traditions. These days he should be regarded as one of *the* original British rock'n' rollers, and one with significant international influence. His uncompromising, nasal singing style and unbridled whoopin' and hollerin' was far more raw than the polished Tommy Steele and Cliff Richard who were to follow. The kids copied him in their thousands. Almost every musician from the forthcoming 'beat boom' could trace their love of music to hearing the great Lonnie Donegan, including members of The Quarrymen, soon to become better known as The Beatles.

Back in Glasgow another genuine innovator was Alex Harvey from Kinning Park. With music in his blood, here was a livewire constantly striving and searching for new styles. At first Harvey sang country, then played jazz trumpet, before eventually embracing rock'n' roll in the Kansas City Skiffle Band and the

Lonnie Donegan arriving for a rehearsal at the Alhambra, Glasgow, *c.*1960s

short-lived Alex Harvey Skiffle Group. Here was the perfect wild frontman, the living embodiment of Scottish rock'n'roll. When the *Daily Record* ran a 'Find Scotland's Tommy Steele' competition in 1956, Harvey won with ease.

At the beginning of the 1960s it was obvious that Scottish music had developed a close kinship with Black American music. Perhaps it was the shared experience of struggle or suffering, or the blues that working-class people felt on either side of the Atlantic. Like Scotland's indigenous folk music, soul music relied on strong melody, advanced musicianship and a powerful voice to make it connect. Perhaps more than elsewhere in the United Kingdom at that time, soul, rhythm'n'blues and blues infiltrated the sound of virtually every new Scottish act.

While Harvey's brother Leslie played a mean guitar in the Kinning Park Ramblers and latterly the Blues Council, it was Alex Harvey and His Soul Band, formed in 1959, that took the club scene by storm, performing originals and covers. These included *Shout* by the Isley Brothers, later made world-famous by a diminutive Scottish lassie we'll hear more about below. The band soon made a considerable reputation for itself playing clubs nationwide, including a weekly residency in Glasgow's La Cave.

London's attitude to rock'n'roll in Scotland was muted to say the least, regarding the country as something of a backwater. Scottish artists who achieved notable success at this time were mostly confined to the novelty shelves. Jackie Dennis, for example, played a sort of rock'n'roll in a kilt, securing number five in the British charts with *La De Da* in 1958. Dennis played the Perry Como television show in the States, then sank without a trace. Lord Rockingham's XI released the raucous

Alex Harvey (left) with Tommy Steele

Photographer unknown
Image by kind permission of Martin Kielty

single *Hoots Mon*, written by band-leader Harry Robinson, which reached number one in 1958. Karl Denver showcased his falsetto yodel on the fourth-placed *Wimoweh* in 1962, but had less success with follow-up singles and albums. Then there was Andy Stewart's *Donald Where's Yer Troosers?* which went into the top forty in 1960 and all the way to number ten when re-released in 1989. All seemed like parodies or light-hearted fluff.

Away from the mainstream, Ricky Barnes ended up in the German city of Hamburg for over a decade, running the Top Ten Club, with Alex Harvey following on; the rest of The Soul Band came over in 1963. As with The Beatles, the Hamburg experience helped to develop the Scottish groups, working on a constant gig schedule with occasional studio recordings. Alex Harvey and His Soul Band soon signed to Polydor and released a pioneering, epony-

mous debut album of driving rhythm'n'blues. Although it was a great collection, it was largely ignored. This was quickly followed by an acoustic album, *The Blues,* featuring Harvey's brother Leslie – which also disappeared from view. Sadly The Soul Band dissolved and Alex returned from Germany to play in Glasgow clubs and ballrooms, frustrated at his lack of progress.

Biting the bullet, Harvey moved to London and joined the production of the controversial rock musical 'Hair'. Another solo album *Roman Wall Blues* followed on Philips/Phonogram, featuring a full band and brass section, with Leslie Harvey in tow once again. But with success still eluding him, Alex Harvey went underground and didn't reappear until the following decade.

At the very start of the 1960s, as the first wave of rock'n'roll began to fade,

Alex Harvey (front) and His Soul Band, 28 October 1964

Photograph by Tony Gale
Pictorial Press Ltd / Alamy Stock Photo

little seemed to be happening in Scotland – but things were about to change. The global impact of The Beatles, The Rolling Stones and the British 'beat boom' was imminent and Scotland soon had its own burgeoning scene. Taking influence from the original '50s rockers and from skiffle, The Shadows, Motown, Stax and American rhythm'n'blues, teenagers in every town grabbed guitars and got to work. Beatlemania was about to break out, with the group's Scottish tour in 1963 beginning in Elgin, Moray, on 2 January. If The Beatles could make it, anyone could give it a go. The possibilities of the '60s seemed within reach for youth and young alike.

Local entrepreneurs, managers and booking agents set up independent record labels, as new nightclubs began to appear across towns and cities. Soon there was a Scotland-wide magazine *Beat News*, and the country's very own pirate station, Radio Scotland, which broadcasted from Hogmanay 1965 until August 1967 aboard the ship 'Comet' in the Firth of Forth, before sailing to other Scottish waterways. Fondly remembered alongside its own *242 Magazine*, the station was a lifeline for the emerging culture.

Members of The Beatles (left to right)
John Lennon, Ringo Starr and Paul
McCartney, Caird Hall, Dundee, 1964

© National Museums Scotland

There were a vast number of amateur and professional acts in Scotland by the mid-'60s, though only a few stood out for their commercial success or influence. Without these pioneers the following decades of popular Scottish music could not have happened and London slowly began to turn its head towards Scotland, sensing hidden treasure north of the border. As the beat boom echoed across the UK, labels such as Decca, CBS and Polydor snapped up northern talent, sometimes releasing only a single or two. It was then up to the bands, managers and record-buying public to determine which acts would go on to establish long-lasting careers. Some did, but most did not.

Driven by original songwriters George Gallacher and Hume Paton, The Poets were true rhythm'n'blues and blues enthusiasts in Glasgow who loved the American singers Howlin' Wolf, Lightnin' Hopkins and Little Walter. Dressed in full Rabbie Burns attire, they had already created a following and were regulars at Glasgow's Flamingo Ballroom when The Rolling Stones' manager Andrew Loog Oldham came to investigate. After a swift audition The Poets were soon in London recording their haunting, twelve-string guitar saturated debut single *Now We're Thru*. Reaching number thirty, they followed it up with the freak-beat masterpiece *That's The Way It's Got To Be*, which didn't chart. When Oldham made it clear that he favoured The Rolling Stones, The Poets were moved from Decca to Immediate and regrettably faded from view. Moving back to Glasgow, they continued to find success on the local scene, though singer George Gallacher eventually left the band. After countless versions of the group with different members, The Poets ended up playing cover versions in clubs to lesser acclaim before finally disbanding. Ex-members such as Hughie Nicolson and Fraser Watson went on to infiltrate other bands such as Marmalade, Blue and Trash.

Another Glasgow band, The Beatstalkers, soon to be christened the Scottish Beatles, had a set that consisted of some originals, obscure American rhythm'n'blues and lots of soul. They struck a genuine mod look and attitude, giving the Small Faces a run for their money in the fuzz and ferocity stakes. The Beatstalkers built up a fanatical following, with an infamous near riot at a free concert in Glasgow's George Square that did much to stoke the hyperbole surrounding the group.

Their Decca single *Ev'rybody's Talking 'Bout My Baby* (1965) sold a whopping 50,000 copies, predominantly in Scotland. However, like other Scottish groups, The Beatstalkers found it near impossible to connect with the London industry and reach English fans, despite tours and an appearance on Rediffusion television's 'Ready Steady Go'. After further singles, including *Silver Tree Top School For Boys* – written by David Bowie who featured on backing vocals – the band had its van and equipment stolen and called it a day in 1969. Years later bass-player Alan Mair would go on to become a key member of new-wave heroes The Only Ones with Peter Perrett, but it was a sold-out Beatstalkers reunion show at the Glasgow Barrowlands in 2005 that truly cemented their homegrown legacy.

Local beat heroes Dean Ford & the Gaylords, named after a Chicago street gang, centred around the clear-cut vocals of Ford underpinned by the sweet harmonies of the band. The Gaylords were friendly rivals of The Poets in Glasgow, releasing singles for the Columbia label in 1964 and 1965. However, amounting to little outside Scotland they became friends of The Tremeloes in 1966, changed their name to The Marmalade and moved south to get involved in the London scene. Soon Jimi Hendrix was claiming fan status. After trial and error The Marmalade had a top-ten single with *Lovin' Things*, followed by dropping the definite article from their name and scoring a number-one hit in January 1969 with John Lennon and Paul McCartney's *Ob-La-Di, Ob-La-Da*. Marmalade was the first Scottish act to go top of the UK charts, and the song was performed at a New Year's Eve special on BBC1. The next single, *Reflections Of My Life* (1969), scored a massive global radio hit that went to number ten in the States and charted all round the world. The band, with central members slowly leaving the fold, continued until 1976 before disappearing from view.

Outwith Glasgow and Edinburgh, Tayside enjoyed a thriving scene of musicians and gig-goers. Willie Wilson and the Down Beats led the local soul scene, but it was the Poor Souls from Dundee who made the grade, releasing on the ALP label and recording a single for Decca. They also supported The Beatles, played in Hamburg and Italy, and were considered some of the finest interpreters of authentic rhythm'n'-blues in the country at that time. The Vikings from Perth, a soul-inspired group with three vocalists, likewise moved to London and played intermittently in Germany. Alan

Opposite: The Beatstalkers, *c.*1960s

Image by kind permission of Martin Kielty

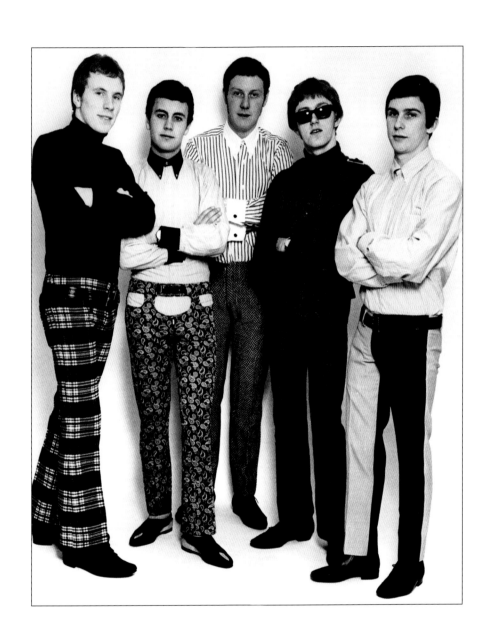

Gorrie, who would go on to play in the Average White Band, featured among their various line-ups.

Beat mentions should go to Banff-based Johnny and the Copycats, who morphed into My Dear Watson. Two singles were released on Parlophone, the first written by George Young of The Easybeats, brother of Angus and Malcolm of AC/DC, and the second featuring Reg Dwight, a.k.a. Elton John, on keyboards. Edinburgh's Boston Dexters were another rhythm'n'blues combo, styling themselves as American gangsters. They moved to London, released two singles and returned to Edinburgh to split. Blues growler Tam White, a member of the band, went on to release singles for Decca in a long, distinguished career as a musician, television host and actor. The Pathfinders were also hot property by 1967. This Glasgow band relocated to London and signed to The Beatles' Apple label. Changing their name to White Trash, later reduced to Trash, they released *Golden Slumbers/Carry That Weight*, a cover of the Abbey Road classic which angered McCartney and pleased Lennon.

You would be right in thinking there is a distinct lack of women around. At

The Marmalade (left to right), with Junior Campbell, Dean Ford, Speccy Graham, Alan Whitehead and Pat Fairley, *c.*1967

grassroots level in the '50s and '60s, women were not as heavily involved in the music scene as today. But as the decades passed this would slowly begin to change. A few did break the 1960s mould, however, including The McKinleys, the sister duo Sheila and Jeanette, who often dressed in tartan. They released four singles for EMI using a 'wall of sound' cavernous reverb. Though lacking a hit as such, they did appear on the television shows 'Ready Steady Go' and 'Thank Your Lucky Stars'.

One female singer who would become a household name – perhaps one of the most successful Scottish singers ever – was 16-year-old Dennistoun schoolgirl Marie McDonald McLaughlin Lawrie, better known as Lulu. Initially part of The Gleneagles, the band was renamed Lulu and the Luvvers, giving the young, bluesy, rock'n'roll singer star billing. Signed to Decca in February 1964, her debut single *Shout* went top ten. The song that had been synonymous with Alex Harvey in Scotland at this time now belonged to her – and still does. A solo career beckoned for Lulu, delivering a strong debut album *Something To Shout About* and a series of slightly less successful follow-up singles. Nonetheless, her career was on an upward trajectory with hit film

The McKinleys, Sheila and Jeanette, 1963

Photograph by Tony Gale
Pictorial Press Ltd / Alamy Stock Photo

theme songs *To Sir With Love* and Bond movie *Man With The Golden Gun*, a winning entry in the 1969 Eurovision Song Contest with *Boom Bang-A-Bang* and successive television and radio shows. Add to that collaborations with David Bowie, Bobby Womack, Elton John and Take That, her charity work, and appearances in shows like 'Absolutely Fabulous', Lulu continues to enjoy success in the business to this day.

As the beat bands bubbled away, other genres of music emerged to capture the hearts of the more thoughtful, introspective teenagers across the land, with many searching for unpretentious, authentic music to soundtrack the decade. The counter-culture was now rearing up in support of civil rights, radical feminism, anti-war protests, the anti-nuclear movement, free love and psychoactive drug use.

Thanks to the unadorned sounds of Bob Dylan, Pete Seeger and Joan Baez, some favoured the strum of an acoustic guitar with pure melody and a sincere, story-telling voice. Hence the 'folk revival'. Inspired in part by English folk singer Ewan McColl and folk archivist Alan Lomax, the musicians Archie Fisher, Hamish Imlach and the guitarist extraordinaire Davy Graham gathered in pubs across Edinburgh to

Lulu, Billy J Kramer and Carol Bingwall,
1960

further the reach of traditional music. For a young, hip audience, this upsurge of singers and guitarists placed Scottish, English and Irish folk songs next to the newer Americana being showcased on the other side of the pond. Graham's 1964 album *Folk, Blues and Beyond*, a collection of Dylan, Lead Belly and Big Bill Broonzy covers, was to prove important and influential.

Bert Jansch discovered these folk singers while sitting in the audience at The Howff Club in Edinburgh. Casting aside his love of beat music, he immersed himself in this new world of traditional music and obsessively frequented folk nights in the city, entranced by Imlach and Graham in particular. Nimbly navigating his way around a guitar and stealing tricks from previous masters, he took Davy Graham's

instrumental *Angi* and made it his own. Since then the piece has been copied by guitar-players the world over. Making the predictable move to London, albums *Bert Jansch* and *It Don't Bother Me* were released in 1965, before he teamed up with another excellent guitarist, John Renbourn. The Pentangle quintet was formed in 1968, with Jacquie McShee, Danny Thomson and Terry Cox. Producing a string of commercially successful albums and consequent solo offerings, Pentangle eventually went their separate ways, but the original line-up was briefly re-formed in 2008 to much acclaim. Pentangle's influence can still be heard as the baroque, acoustic, folk-influenced pop music style continues to ebb and flow.

Another local lad who had been through beat groups, jazz bands and art-school experimentalism, was a Dylan devotee by the name of Mike Heron. Launching a folk night at the Crown Bar on Lothian Street, Edinburgh, Heron connected with multi-instrumentalist Robin Williamson, releasing a song on the *Edinburgh Folk Festival*

Bert Jansch, folk guitarist, 1968

1965 album. Heron and Williamson expanded into a trio with English banjo-player Clive Palmer, moving to Glasgow to start the all-night Clive's Incredible Folk Club which attracted other aspiring musicians such as John Martyn. Here the trio would derive their own name, The Incredible String Band. A truly inimitable endeavour, they mixed up traditional folk, Americana and psychedelia. The term 'freak folk' was coined, deemed fitting for this new freewheeling form of acoustic expression.

American producer Joe Boyd signed the trio to Elektra Records in 1966 and released their first album. After a brief hiatus in Morocco and Afghanistan, with Palmer departing the band, Heron and Williamson made the sprawling, ethnic-influenced *The 5000 Spirits Or The Layers Of The Onion* (1967), followed by the critically lauded *The Hangman's Beautiful Daughte*r and *Big Tam And The Wee Huge* (1968).

Although Williamson and Heron's song-styles were markedly different, they

worked together to transcend their folk roots and embed themselves as pioneers of the counter-culture. The band played the Woodstock festival, toured the States, introduced audiences to 'world music' and packed out halls, far exceeding the expectations of their early jam-session roots. Reigning supreme for a few years they disbanded in 1974 after eight albums, only to re-form in 1999 – much to the appreciation of a new generation of fans.

Donovan Leitch was born and bred in Glasgow and lived there until the age of ten. Though moving down south after that time, his music harked back to his Scottish roots.

He was discovered by chance playing folk songs in St Albans and signed to Pye Records in 1964. Only a year later he found himself in the top five. Blessed with good looks, and a sartorial style of peaked cap and denims,

The Incredible String Band, Mike Heron
(left) and Robin Williamson (right), 1968

Pictorial Press Ltd / Alamy Stock Photo

Donovan was a British folk artist at the same time Bob Dylan was connecting with audiences in America. His debut album *What's Bin Did And What's Bin Hid* may have been seen as Dylan-esque, but on the second album *Fairytale* Donovan developed his own whimsical style and embraced psychedelia, myth and childlike themes, though he had problems balancing pop-stardom with a sense of authenticity as some folk purists claimed it wasn't the 'real deal'.

After contractual wrangling in 1966, Donovan went to number one of the Billboard Hot 100 in the States with *Sunshine Superman*. The star shone bright and his legend was assured. In hindsight his albums are true snapshots of the swingin' '60s and still sound utterly alive today.

Even by 1968, as the beat scene was transforming, psychedelia had not yet hit Scotland. People wanted to dance rather than sit and stroke their chins, and nightclubs still enjoyed beat and soul bands. Young Edinburgh rockers The Jury decided to find their 'third eye' however, and transformed into Writing on the Wall. With charismatic singer Linnie Paterson up front, they blended folk, rock and psychedelia into

Donovan at the International Jazz Festival, 1968

a dynamic if slightly unusual live act. BBC Radio 1 disc jockey John Peel championed the group and like many Scots before them they made the move to London, aiming for a welcome into the hippie mecca Middle Earth club. Despite support from the BBC and live audiences, their album *The Power Of The Picts* did them no favours and the band quit when their instruments were stolen.

Eclipsing everyone's success from Scotland throughout the '60s was a certain John Symon Asher Bruce. Born into a musical family from Bishopbriggs, East Dunbartonshire, Bruce attended the Royal Scottish Academy of Music and Drama on a cello and double bass scholarship, but was eventually asked to leave on account of his fanatical love of jazz. Moving to London he joined bands such as the acclaimed Blues Incorporated and Graham Bond Quartet, beside drummer and future arch-nemesis Ginger Baker, where his bass-playing skills were duly noticed and soon revered. After successful stints in The Bluesbreakers and Manfred Mann, it was as part of the power-trio Cream, with Eric Clapton and Baker at his side, that Jack Bruce would become a household name in 1966. Cream's jazz-inflected, blues-based testimony doffed its cap

Cream, (left to right) Ginger Baker, Jack
Bruce and Eric Clapton, 1968

to the all-engulfing psychedelia of the time and the band became standard-bearers of an unhindered 'hard rock' that would blossom further over the next decade and beyond. Touring the world, winning awards, entering the annals as the first 'super-group' and selling millions of copies of their four classic albums – Cream did *everything* in a very short space of time, splitting by the end of 1968. Audiences, critics and fellow musicians adored them. Their third opus *Wheels Of Fire* topped the charts in the States, becoming the first platinum double album.

Bruce, one of psychedelic rock's main journeymen, co-wrote and sang most of Cream's best-known compositions and would inspire generations to come. Although best-loved for his work in the group, he was a professional musician who played jazz, blues, pop, folk and world music over six decades and left an indelible mark. Music would never be the same, due in part to Jack Bruce and his virtuosic, soulful style.

It was certainly true that some Scottish artists were now enjoying enormous success, but only those who had decided to uproot themselves to make the move to London. This was a trend that would continue throughout the '50s and '60s until the end of the '90s. As in the worlds of entertainment, film, television and media, the vast majority of writers, actors and broadcasters also relocated to the Big Smoke to further their careers. Although a few stoically stayed put for the long haul, it was seen as impossible, almost laughable, to remain in Scotland and carve out a successful career. The country was still regarded as a cultural backwater.

But as pop music's most wide-eyed decade drew to a close, Scottish musicians were more connected to the global heartbeat than ever. As well as music itself, local enthusiasts and aficionados were digging into the new rock'n'roll counter-culture and developing it on their home turf. As the 1970s loomed the country was in flux. Both hardship and heroism would lie ahead for Scotland's musicians as they moved further towards pop-culture's nucleus. There was a *lot* more to come.

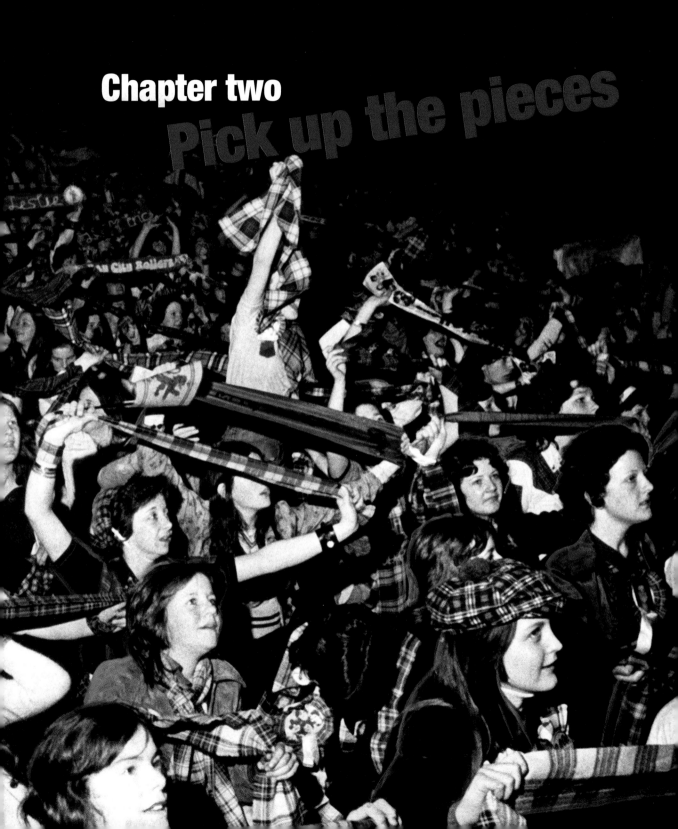

Chapter two

Pick up the pieces

At the start of the 1970s pop music had eased into its third decade and embedded itself in the global consciousness. Like it or not, something seen as little more than a teenage fad had become a major cultural barometer and an enormous worldwide industry. Its major stars could now command the largest global audiences in history, while their news and views attracted enormous publicity. The '70s are often remembered as a decade of glamour, excess and debauchery. Garish fashions, conceptual ideas, outlandish recording techniques and the pharmaceutically-assisted leisure activities that surrounded the music business had developed far beyond its humble, somewhat naive beginnings. Global tastes and fashions were changing and pop music began to splinter into multiple genres. This was the decade of flares, lapels, glitz, glitter, disco, funk – and in Scotland, lots of tartan.

But at the beginning of the decade, progressive rock ruled the roost in T-shirt and jeans, eschewing the showbiz of before. Gone were the clean-cut, be-suited, cheeky chappies of the previous decade, replaced by a far earthier, bearded, long-haired equivalent. Rock'n'roll was now being presented as more intellectual, with serious political opinions and a worthiness missing from the groups of the past twenty years. To be 'pop' in itself wasn't enough for some, and in many ways it was the opposite of the zeitgeist. Perhaps this had something to do with the times. The euphoria of the 1960s and the promise of a better life seemed less likely, due in part to the reality of impending financial woes and political upheaval gathering on the horizon. But despite the fluctuation of governments and politics, Scotland's musicians quietly beavered away, looking to compete on the world stage. The '60s beat boom now seemed outdated; experimentation and further exploration of blues, jazz, folk and Americana was now the order of the day.

London may have been at the cutting edge and continuously searching for new inspiration, but this did not always chime with Scottish audiences. As pot-smoking musicians put their heads down, turned up the amplifiers and riffed away, the dance hall-friendly sounds of soul and rhythm'n'blues dwindled – as did the audiences.

**Pages 20–21: The crowd goes crazy at a
Bay City Rollers concert, 1975**

Life was hard for the working classes in Scotland and people wanted to party rather than sit on the floor cross-legged. These more cerebral acts didn't necessary soundtrack a wild weekend. Having said that, a thread does run through almost all Scottish acts of the '70s, no matter what genre they inhabited. The emphasis was on melodies and hooks; whether pure pop or hard rock, the song was key.

Watching the brightest and best talent disappear to London was tough though. As the thriving Scottish club scene of the 1960s slowly dissolved, promoters threw in their lot and venues closed across the country. The new prog and experimental bands tended to be booked by universities and colleges, dividing audiences even further. Some of these acts also appeared more aloof and even disconnected from the crowd. Add into the mix the rise of gang violence in Glasgow from the Tongs and the Fleeto, and a Friday and Saturday night on the tiles looked less enticing.

The hippest hangout for musicians at the time was the Burns Howff in West Regent Street, Glasgow, seen as the epicentre of the local, working-man's hard rock scene. A few prog rock bands did manage to build an audience at home across the Central Belt, but an act called 1-2-3, who moved to London in 1967, briefly became the talk of the town as a result of a residency at The Marquee. Their blend of organ, bass and drums paved the way for Keith Emerson and Rick Wakeman's excursions, and attracted plaudits from Pete Townsend and David Bowie among others. Signing to the newly-founded Chrysalis label they were renamed Clouds, released two albums fusing prog and pop, and toured extensively. Still seen as innovators their star shone brightly for the hip *cognoscenti*, but fizzled out by 1971.

Another notable band of the era was Cartoone, who morphed from their previous name The Chevlons and once again made the move to London. With help from Lulu acolyte Mark London, they managed to get their songs to Atlantic Records who signed them several months before they took on Led Zeppelin. With Jimmy Page on guest guitar, Cartoone released a debut album and supported Led Zeppelin in the USA, with a certain Leslie Harvey on guitar. The Chevlons were then unceremoniously dropped by the label and disappeared from view – such was the fickle world they inhabited.

Leslie Harvey was on loan from a band who would have slightly more impact

locally and internationally before coming to a heart-breaking end. Stone the Crows, originally from Glasgow and known as Power, featured the soulful vocals of bassist Jimmy Dewar (Lulu and the Luvvers) and lead singer Maggie Bell. Bell was a Mary-hill girl who had sung with the Kinning Park Ramblers alongside Harvey on guitar, and then in various house bands across Glasgow's dance halls. Dewar, Harvey and Bell worked well together and the new band's heavier sound eventually came to the attention of Led Zep manager Peter Grant who agreed to manage them. With Harvey's sinuous guitar-playing and Bell's bluesy howl, they drew worthy comparison to Janis Joplin and soon developed their own brand of rock with a fluctuating line-up. Having three albums and a red-hot live show under their belt by 1972, the future looked relatively rosy until the disastrous and fatal onstage electrocution of Harvey in Swansea Top Rank. Though they attempted to soldier on, the band folded in 1973. Maggie Bell continued as a solo artist with massive potential, albeit to diminishing returns, earning herself a deserved reputation as one of the country's great blues vocalists.

Stone the Crows, with Maggie Bell, 1972

Trinity Mirror / Mirrorpix / Alamy Stock
Photo

Perhaps the biggest success story of Scotland's early '70s hard rock scene was a quartet from Dunfermline in Fife known as Nazareth. Pilfering their name from a lyric in *The Weight* sung by American country-rockers The Band, they transformed themselves from '60s beat aficionados The Shadettes with the original line-up almost intact. Dan McCafferty, Pete Agnew and Daryll Sweet had come together in 1960 and over a decade later were beginning to reap the rewards in this new incarnation – showing real perseverance. After two misfired albums recorded in London, their third, *Razamanaz* (1973), connected with the record-buying public and produced two top-ten hits in *Bad Bad Boy* and *Broken Down Angel*. For the next few years their melodic, anthemic and commercially viable take on hard rock made them a global sensation. Their self-produced album *Hair Of The Dog,* produced at their peak in 1975, has been a staple for dedicated rock fans ever since.

Nazareth toured the world, hit the top ten in the States with a version of *Love Hurts,* had global number-one hits with originals and well-placed covers, eventually seeing *Hair Of The Dog* performed by rock behemoths Guns'n'Roses in 1994 on *The*

Nazareth performing in Scotland, *c.*1977

Spaghetti Incident album. But from the late '70s onwards, the band's fortunes declined – although they continue to tour for devoted audiences today with Agnew the sole original member.

Almost every Scottish musician who would attain any kind of fame, fortune, acclaim or kudos over the new decade had a lineage that ran from the 1960s. Rock'n'roll was still in its relative infancy, so craftsmanship and endurance were earned and respected. Any fairweather part-timers would soon fall by the wayside, while true campaigners would slowly reap the benefits of their hard work and dedication. If the music of the original beat scene died with the previous decade, the musicians certainly had not. Scottish artists, like those the world over, transformed and developed their work to remain relevant, hip and happening.

Another vocalist who easily straddled the worlds of soul and rock, building up a fervent following, was Frankie Miller. Hailing from Bridgeton, Glasgow, Miller performed in the groups The Del-Jacks and Sock 'em JB before teaming up with Jimmy Doris (who would go on to write for Lulu and others) in The Stoics, a rock band with serious talent and potential. Having moved to London like everyone else, Miller joined another group, Jude, for a brief period before going solo.

As a reaction to the overblown, impenetrable world of prog rock, a new grassroots form developed that would earn the unenviable title of 'pub rock'. Miller was attracted to its no-nonsense attitude and passion for country, soul and early rock'n'roll. He began to hang out with nascent scenesters Eggs Over Easy and eventually recorded his debut album *Once In A Blue Moon* with mainstays Brinsley

Frankie Miller, December 1975

Trinity Mirror / Mirrorpix / Alamy Stock
Photo

Schwartz. Miller's next move was to have his album *High Life* produced by the New Orleans soul legend Allen Toussaint. Miller was now ready to hit his stride, crafting songs and cultivating his rugged voice. The triumph came in 1975 with album *The Rock*, including a top-ten spot with *Darlin'* and an appearance on a Thin Lizzy album performing a duet with Phil Lynott, *Still In Love With You*.

Though never a hugely visible star who regularly bothered the charts, Miller's gritty, soulful voice was heralded as one of the best in rock'n'roll. Rod Stewart claimed it could bring a tear to the eye. In truth Miller's songs may be better known than his work as a performer, having been covered by international artists including Ray Charles, Johnny Cash, Roy Orbison, Etta James and The Eagles. On his home turf his rendition of folk singer Dougie Maclean's *Caledonia* in 1992 was a hit and is often cited as the definitive version. Sadly Frankie Miller's career was cut short in 1994 when he suffered a brain haemorrhage, waking from a coma five months later unable to speak or sing. Fans and friends keep a torch lit in honour of his undeniable talent.

In the early '70s hard rock may have had something of a stranglehold on the music press, scenesters and universities across the land, but other forms of music were reaching their maturity. Scotland's deep love of Black soul music was fully realised in one particular group – the Average White Band. Tayside had been served well in the '60s by Perth soul-boys The Vikings, but they had already beaten a path to London with band leader Alan Gorrie at the forefront. On his unstoppable quest to make proper rhythm'n'blues, Gorrie joined The Scots of St James, who then became Hopscotch and promptly broke up. He then formed another group, Forever More, who released two albums but disbanded by 1971. But Gorrie's stars would soon align on a new project, with the trusted 'Dundee Horns' (Malcolm Duncan and Roger Ball), members of the band Mogul Thrash, and Hamish Stuart from another Scottish band Dream Police. The years of listening, learning and honing their skills as players were finally rewarded. With a name given to them by Gorrie's wife Jean, the Average White Band was an act that had syncopation and swing, which could groove and deliver authentic soulful hooks in abundance.

Debut album *Show Your Hand* arrived on MCA Records in 1973, but had little impact commercially, though it did pave the way for a tour in the States. After a

chance meeting with industry lynchpin Jerry Wexler in 1974, the recently dropped group signed to soul powerhouse Atlantic Records, with his personal seal of approval. As their name suggested, here were mostly skinny white dudes playing Black American music so well that many musicians and listeners in the USA could not believe they were not American. With second album *AWB* (*The White Album*), they hit payola when instrumental masterpiece *Pick Up The Pieces* went to number one in the States and six in the UK, connecting with the new disco crowd. Average White Band was a bonafide soul phenomenon. Sly Stone, Bobby Womack and Mr Dyna-mite himself, James Brown, allegedly gave their blessing to AWB's work and The JBs even recorded a funk repost to their biggest hit. The band had achieved more than they could ever hope for in their beloved genre and *Pick Up The Pieces* is still regarded as a stone-cold, dance-floor classic to this day.

At their peak, however, disaster struck. The band's inimitable, funky drummer Robbie MacIntosh overdosed on heroin at a Los Angeles aftershow party. Legend has it that the band had assumed it was cocaine before imbibing it, and members

Average White Band, *c.*1975

Pictorial Press Ltd / Alamy Stock Photo

of the Hollywood glitterati, including Cher, kept others in the band alive by forcing them to stay awake. This blight on AWB's career wrong-footed them completely and future records were dedicated to MacIntosh's shocking demise. With albums such as *Cut the Cake*, *Soul Searching* and *Feel No Fret* keeping the funk alive and their name in lights throughout the '70s, the band eventually wound down in 1983. Re-forming in 1989, a version of the band featuring the unwavering and steadfast Gorrie continues to lay down the law on a stage near you.

If you think of Scottish pop music, the 1970s and tartan, only one group comes to mind – the Bay City Rollers. Instantly recognisable and massively popular for a brief time in the '70s, it is not so well known that it actually took many years and many line-ups to get there. The absolute antithesis of the earnest and beardy hard rock of the time, they were to become one of the decade's ultimate boy-bands.

Starting out at school in Edinburgh as The Saxons – centred around the brothers Alan and Derek Longmuir – the band were soon taken under the arm of controlling Prestonpans-based manager Tam Paton, a former musician and band-leader himself. Having once met Beatles manager Brian Epstein, who stressed the importance of image, Paton changed their name to Bay City Rollers and put his young charges through their paces every weekend with a clean-cut dress code and a new set of populist chart covers at Edinburgh's Palais de Dance and Top Story Club. They were encouraged to do charity work, not to have girlfriends, and to cultivate a squeaky-clean image. In time the plan worked and the band started to draw bigger local crowds than the touring acts, and demand equal fees for performing.

Trapped in Edinburgh one night by bad weather, Richard Leahy of Bell Records was taken to see the band and was astonished by the queues of young girls screaming for them. The Rollers were signed there and then, with a view to encouraging similar screaming crowds all over Britain. With the guiding hand of the later controversial pop-guru Jonathan King, they secured a top-ten hit with *Keep On Dancing* in 1973, but failed to capitalise on their success. With a revolving door of twenty-seven different members passing through their ranks as their career developed, the band eventually delivered on their original promise with a new line-up of frontman Les McKeown, guitarists Eric Faulkner and Stuart 'Woody' Wood, alongside the Longmuir brothers.

In their legendary attire of tartan-trimmed bell-bottoms, tartan scarves and feather-cut hair, saccharine hits such as *Remember*, *Bye Bye Baby*, *Shang-A-Lang* and *Give A Little Love* poured out of them. By 1975 they had two albums, their own TV show and were heralded as 'the biggest group since the Beatles'. The hysteria, given the name 'Rollermania', took off at home, Canada, Australia, Japan and America.

But like a comet, the Rollers dive-bombed into obscurity quicker than they had arrived. By 1978 infighting, corruption, controversy, bad business decisions and the continual change of members put paid to the band. They limped into the 1980s with no chart recognition, paltry sales and shrinking crowds. Manager Tam Paton was later imprisoned for indecency and fined for drug-dealing, only one aspect that contributed to a pervading sense of notoriety that surrounded the band. Nonetheless, the Rollers are still fondly remembered by many. When the band re-formed in 2015 they immediately sold out and look set to release a new album. Though not favoured by scenesters or the serious press, the band was one of Scotland's most commercial successes and were truly taken into the hearts of thousands.

Also not the most critically lauded act around, Glasgow quartet Middle of the Road began as Los Caracas and won on the TV talent show 'Opportunity Knocks'. With an Italian producer and name-change, they developed a 'europop' sound to score a series of UK hits, including in 1971 the million-selling number one *Chirpy Chirpy Cheep Cheep*.

With the exception of other acts such as Pilot, with ex-Rollers Davie Paton and Billy Lyall whose *Magic* sold over a million copies, and James 'Midge' Ure's band Slik, Scotland's music tended to reflect the political times and industrial upheaval of the period. The singer-songwriter genre, rooted in the folk circuit, began to take shape in its own right with burgeoning successes on the horizon. While not overtly political as such, these were serious, contemplative writers, like the artist John Martyn. Following a psyche-folk apprenticeship in Glasgow, watching The Incredible String Band and others, he moved to London, played pubs and coffee shops, and signed to Island Records. Solo albums *London Conversation* and *The Tumbler* followed in 1967/68, before he worked with his then wife Beverley on two albums in 1970, establishing his unique Echoplex-driven sound. Martyn's personal lyrical meditations, exquisite guitar-

playing, effortless groove and slurred singing style marked him out as one of the true original singer-songwriters. Martyn incorporated jazz, rock and reggae into his acoustic folk and blues sound, releasing five more albums throughout the 1970s and a total of twenty-one during his career until his death in 2009. Throughout a tumultuous life of wild living, alcoholism and drug abuse, it was his music – and the 1973 album *Solid Air* in particular – that brought him into the homes of millions. His influence can still be heard everywhere.

Barbara Dickson, who came from Dunfermline, began her career singing in Fife folk clubs in 1964 at the age of seventeen. She collaborated on two albums with leading folkie Archie Fisher and performed the first two albums of her solo repertoire in clubs in the '60s and early '70s, becoming a well-respected voice on the British folk scene. In 1973 Dickson took a different direction and entered the world of musical theatre, quickly becoming a genuine mainstream pop singer. Although known for the massive 1980s hit *I Know Him So Well* with Elaine Paige – the bestselling female duet of all time – she also appeared on weekly television and provided backing vocals for

Slik, (left to right) Jim McGinlay, Kenny Hyslop, Midge Ure and Billy McIsaac, London, January 1976

© Martyn Goodacre / Getty Images

Gerry Rafferty on his two biggest solo albums. With approximately thirty albums to her name, various top-twenty singles and critically acclaimed television drama and theatre work, Barbara Dickson is one of the biggest-selling female solo artists to come out of Scotland, receiving an OBE in 2002. Over the last fifteen years she has returned to singing and to folk music, her true love.

Another Fifer who infiltrated the Scottish and London scenes was St Andrews-born Rab Noakes, a Bob Dylan devotee and budding songwriter. Having learned his finger-picking craft in Glasgow, London and his native Cupar, Noakes played the folk circuit with Fisher and Dickson. He also got to know Gerry Rafferty, briefly joining Stealers Wheel. Although never as commercially successful as his peers, Noakes' songs were highly regarded and covered by many, including all the aforementioned. As a solo artist he released albums for Decca, A&M, MCA and Warner Brothers throughout the '70s, and carved out a distinguished career as a senior producer at BBC Radio Scotland throughout the '80s and '90s. Rab Noakes is still making albums and performing live to this day.

John Martyn (left), *c.*1978

Barbara Dickson at the Gateway Studios, Leith, Edinburgh, 18 April 1972

Beloved songwriter and proud Paisley 'buddy', Gerry Rafferty made music that went far and wide. With a lightness of melodic touch and delicate vocal harmonies, his mainly acoustic songwriting led to a partnership with Joe Egan which saw them form the band Fifth Column and release a single for EMI. After their short life-span, Rafferty joined comedic songwriting duo The Humblebums, with musician Tam Harvey and comedian-in-the-making Billy Connolly. When Tam Harvey quit, Rafferty and Connolly brought out two acclaimed albums and toured, with Connolly perfecting his stage banter as Rafferty improved his song-craft and musicianship. As Rafferty was less keen on touring and more enamoured by the studio, The Humblebums eventually split. Rafferty's debut solo album was produced in 1971.

With Noakes briefly at his side, Rafferty formed Stealers Wheel and joined forces once again with Joe Egan. Though signing with A&M in 1972 and working with the famous Jerry Lieber and Mike Stoller writing/production team, the hits did not materialise until the shuffling *Stuck In The Middle With You* went top ten in Britain and the States, with the song used to disturbing effect years later in the cult classic film 'Reservoir Dogs'. They were on a roll and made two more albums before finally quitting because of management problems and the usual artistic differences.

While continuing to contribute to work by others, Rafferty again went solo and enjoyed his greatest success yet. The smooth, soulful albums *City By City* and *Night Owl* were huge hits on both sides of the Atlantic, with the single *Baker Street* and its iconic saxophone motif still an FM rock radio standard today, notching up millions of plays globally.

Although much of his dedicated audience stayed with him through the next

**Billy Connolly (left) with Gerry Rafferty
(right) of The Humblebums, in a Glasgow
pub, 1970**

© The Scotsman Publications Ltd
Licensor www.SCRAN.ac.uk

three decades, Rafferty was an incredibly private person, shunning fame and celebrity. For him it was all about the music. As well as releasing more albums in the '80s, '90s and the 2000s, he produced acts such as The Proclaimers. Struggling with debilitating alcoholism, Gerry Rafferty passed away in 2011 to a massive outpouring of grief and respect from collaborators, friends and fans across the globe.

Gallagher & Lyle were friends and associates of Rafferty, and also hugely significant songwriters. Benny Gallagher and Graham Lyle began their musical lives together as The Tulsans, based in Largs and Saltcoats in North Ayrshire. With Scottish and Irish folk influences, as well as The Everly Brothers and Buddy Holly, they made the inevitable move to London in 1966 after two singles on Decca. They were signed as a songwriting duo to The Beatles' Apple publishing in 1968 and wrote a few B-sides for various Apple artists. Joining the already established McGuinness Flint in 1970, Gallagher and Lyle experienced their first flush of success with the co-written number-two hit *When I'm Dead And Gone*. But sitting uncomfortably in someone else's group, they struck out as a duo in their own right in 1971, producing an easy-listening blend of traditional folk, acoustic pop and sweet harmony. The persistence and determination of the duo saw a real breakthrough on their fifth album *Breakaway* in 1976, featuring soft-focus singles *I Wanna Stay With You* and *Heart On My Sleeve* – possibly the antithesis of the oncoming blitzkrieg of punk rock.

Gallagher & Lyle's songs have been famously covered by Simon & Garfunkel, Bryan Ferry, Ringo Starr, Status Quo and many others over the years, but the duo themselves parted ways in 1980, with touring being cited as incompatible with family life. Lyle went on to form another writing duo with Terry Britten and in this partnership wrote the smash-hit comeback single of Tina Turner – *What's Love Got To Do With It?* Gallagher & Lyle got back together in 2010 with a tour to celebrate.

Renowned as writers and performers, Aberdeenshire folk duo The Sutherland Brothers hit gold with their debut single *(I Don't Want To Love You But) You Got Me Anyway*, but are also famous for penning Rod Stewart's monster-hit *Sailing*. Teaming up with rock band Quiver, they delivered a series of albums and the sing-along *Arms of Mary* in 1976. For fact fans, Quiver bassist Bruce Thomas would go on to join Elvis Costello & The Attractions.

At the opposite end of the spectrum – and to someone who would have a profound effect on what was about to happen next, namely punk rock – we return to rock'n'roll crusader and eternal underdog Alex Harvey. Back in Glasgow from London after performing in the musical 'Hair' and making failed solo albums, Harvey was in search of a new muse. Hard rockers Tear Gas, featuring Zal Cleminson of '60s band Bo Weavils and cousins Hugh and Ted McKenna, had likewise moved to London. But having released two acclaimed but ineffective albums, *Piggy Go Getter* and *Tear Gas*, they too were back in Glasgow cooling their heels, having forsaken a budding career.

Meeting in the Burns Howff in West Regent Street, they took off for a nearby rehearsal room and the synergy between band and singer was instantaneous. Harvey was looking for more dramatic and heavier sounding musicians to back up his new conceptual sound and image. Playing early numbers such as *Midnight Moses*, Cleminson and the McKennas attacked the arrangements and injected them with new life, with Harvey pushing himself and a set of theatrical characters into more aggressive territory. The wildman had always been there in his skiffle, beat and soul years, but now he positively leered at the audience through his new music.

The Sensational Alex Harvey Band,
Reading Rock Festival, August 1977

Lebrecht Music and Arts Photo Library /
Alamy Stock Photo

With a committed work ethic and cast-iron constitution, the new line-up was preposterously named The Sensational Alex Harvey Band. Setting out to wind up crowds wherever they went, Harvey instigated a sense of surrealism, melodrama and the avant-garde that set them aside from the glam and hard rock of the day. He was also fifteen years older than the others in the band, but kept up with their energy and hard-drinking. The band were heavy of course, but also capable of playing songs made famous by French folkie Jacques Brel and Welsh vocalist Tom Jones, among others. Zal Cleminson took to wearing panstick mime-artist make-up onstage, with Harvey doing his leering up front, adorned in a striped pirate's shirt and curly locks. They looked as weird as they sounded. At first, audiences didn't know what to make of them, but the camaraderie, inclusiveness and cynical in-jokes enticed and engulfed an army of fanatics. In some ways, they were punk before punk.

Never quite living up to their live show, however, the band unleashed a series of eight idiosyncratic and often remarkable records between *Framed* (1972) and *Rock Drill* (1978), scoring two top-forty hits in *Delilah* and *Boston Tea Party*, as well as appearing on 'Top of the Pops'. Their cult following ensured sell-out tours and rapturous devotion from the converted, but proved to be slightly too odd for mainstream acceptance, and success in the States alluded them. The band folded at the end of the '70s and Harvey managed to release two solo albums before his unforeseen heart attack at forty-six years old in 1982, on tour in Belgium. He'd felt strong enough to tour, having suffered only a little recent ill health, but years of rock'n'roll living since the '50s had taken its toll. It was the end of an extraordinary life and career – that of a true pioneer and innovator.

As the 1970s drew to a close, Scotland's musical profile across Britain, and indeed the world, was strengthening. Against a backdrop of industrial decline, strikes, unemployment and civil unrest, Scottish musicians had encompassed the serious and sensuous, as well as the eccentric and populist elements of modern life. London may have drawn the majority of talent down south, but the inspiration, musicianship and melodic dexterity of those who had succeeded provided motivation for future Scottish artists. Nevertheless, the next generation wanted to rip it all up and start again.

Chapter three
Treasure

Recorded music has only existed for the relatively short period of about 160 years, and the gramophone disc for even less. Folk today have lived their entire lives surrounded by recorded music in one shape or form. As we enter a new era when almost all music ever recorded can be digitally streamed via the internet – as simple as turning on a water tap – it is interesting to look at our relationship with the physical artefacts themselves and the ways in which we acquire our music.

Merchandise has always been central to pop for artists and fans alike. T-shirts,

scarves, badges, posters, programmes – and of course the records themselves – are essential to keep the wheels of industry turning. Nothing proves a fan's dedication more than a full set of band memorabilia. It can be tribal and identity driven, but it also commemorates well-loved artists in a fun and financially lucrative way. The revenue allows musicians to create their art, to tour the world and live their lives. Today's fans have ring-tones, computer apps and interactive games to entice them, with personal 'meet and greet' opportunities, back-stage passes and signing sessions making the interface between artist and audience closer than ever. It's perhaps a bit more complicated than acquiring a tartan scarf or button badge.

The song itself is hugely personal. It can reflect or represent a specific time in our lives, success or failure, hardship or joy, heartbreak or true love. Many of us keep a record of those memories and emotions, times and places –

Pages 38–39: Lots of vinyl records

Twin Design / Shutterstock.com

Chantal Meteor jukebox, Bristol, England, 1959–62

© National Museums Scotland

hence music collections become such an intimate chronicle of our lives. As well as the music, some of us are even attached to the formats themselves. Since the dawn of pop, as technology has advanced and consumer habits changed, we've enjoyed our favourite songs on vinyl, cassette tape, compact disc, digital download and now as streams. Although a more niche concern, vinyl is experiencing a renaissance these days, probably due to the sound quality, tactile nature of the object and sheer nostalgia. As collectors spend enormous sums globally on original vinyl, pressing plants are once again booming with rekindled demand.

Record shops have also played a major role in sustaining local music scenes throughout the years and are more than merely outlets for flogging merchandise. Though many of these communities have since moved online, shops have always been at the forefront of each new musical movement, endorsing and nurturing musicians as well as educating the public. The spaces themselves become crucibles for like-minded souls, networking musicians and local gig promotion. Before the internet the only genuine portals of music discovery were the music press, radio, and

Leafing through albums at the Other Record Shop, Princes Street, Edinburgh, 1985

© The Scotsman Publication Ltd
Licensor www.SCRAN.ac.uk

going to the local shop. Although chainstores like HMV, Virgin, Our Price, Tower and Fopp have served the public well, it was, and still is, the independent outlets that offer a more personal and unique experience. These shops stock the weird and wonderful, opening a window into another world for the customer, casual browser and curious teenager. Leafing through the dusty racks, looking at the poster-strewn walls, eavesdropping on hipster con-versations at the counter, are essential for any avid music fan.

Not many outlets have developed a reputation beyond their lifetime, but Bruce's Record shops have. Perhaps it was the era, attention to detail, dedication to the local scene, or the memorable red bags stating 'I Found It At Bruce's'. Opened in 1967 in Falkirk by the budding entrepreneur Bruce Findlay and his brother Brian, the Edinburgh branch of Bruce's Records arrived in 1969 and became a hub for those interested in the new sights, sounds and scenes. Bruce's shops spread across Scotland, inspiring others to do something similar until well into the 1980s. Like gig venues and bands themselves, Bruce's and the shops that followed would become trusted institutions and pillars of the underground community.

There are still record shops across the world, albeit in dwindling numbers with increasingly small margins. As a music-mad nation, Scotland is no different. Each town, city or decent-sized metropolis has a shop to shout about. As many have fallen by the wayside, honorary mentions must go to Avalanche and Ripping in Edinburgh, John Smith's, 23rd Precinct and Missing in Glasgow, Chalmers & Joy in Dundee, One Up in Aberdeen, Imperial Music in Inverness and Sleeves in Kirkcaldy. All were won-derful 'bricks and mortar' establishments that couldn't quite surf the digital wave,

Bruce Findlay outside his record shop in Edinburgh, 1969

pay the rent and keep the records in the racks. Some have survived, thankfully, and new ones are appearing. Scotland's oldest record outlet, Concorde Records in Perth, has recently celebrated fifty years of business. Groucho's in Dundee is over forty and still going strong with new, second-hand product and concert ticket sales. And Edinburgh's Vinyl Villains has recently reached its thirty-fifth birthday.

Glasgow's Monorail opened in 2002, demonstrating how a modern experience could be achieved. Run by Stephen Pastel and friends, this independently-minded, eclectic operation sees an array of stock housed next to a bar, restaurant, gig venue and gallery space called Mono. Dance, urban and electronic music is expertly catered for by Rubadub in Glasgow and Underground Solu'shn in Edinburgh. Coda will look after your folk, traditional and Americana needs. And the indie flag flies at Voxbox and Love Music, also in Scotland's two main cities.

Scour the country for new and used bargains and you'll find Unknown Pleasures in Edinburgh, Assai in Dundee and Edinburgh, LP Records in Glasgow, Barnstorm in Dumfries, Big Sparra Vinyl in Ayr, Feel the Groove in Paisley, Europa Music in Stirling, Mo Fidelity in Montrose, Union Vinyl in Inverness, and MaidinVinyl, Chameleon and Spin in Aberdeen. The record shop's demise is not yet a done deal.

With artists and retailers firmly in place, the middleman has always been the label. Scotland's geographical position was doubtless an obstacle to setting up this important cornerstone of the business, though being far from industry centres like London, Berlin, New York or Los Angeles hasn't stopped people trying. Back in the '60s there were a number of independent record labels in Scotland, including Norco run by Albert Bonici (the first label), Thomas Bryce Laing's Waverley and ALP owned by Andy Lothian. In the '70s Lenny Love set up Edinburgh's first independent punk label Sensible Records to release The Rezillos' first single *Can't Stand My Baby*; and the aforementioned Bruce Findlay founded Zoom Records to unleash new-wave delights by The Valves, Cheetahs and PVC2 (previously Slik, featuring Midge Ure).

Most impressive of all was a young troublemaker Bob Last, once a roadie but by then manager of The Rezillos, who founded Fast Product. Focusing on the product to an incredible level of detail – the artwork, packaging, design and marketing of releases – Last issued debuts by both local and non-Scottish acts. Fast Product soon stood next to Rough Trade and Factory as a beacon of ambition, innovation and independence, until Last eventually got bored. His next venture was Pop:Aural which concentrated on Scottish bands, such as Boots for Dancing and the Fire Engines, but this was soon abandoned for music management and a career in the film industry.

Somewhat in competition with Fast Product, Alan Horne hailed 'The Sound of Young Scotland' as coming from the West End of Glasgow via Postcard Records. From 1979, for approximately eighteen months or so, Horne famously issued only twelve records – for Orange Juice, Josef K, The Go Betweens and Aztec Camera, plus one album release – before letting go of Postcard. His next project, Swamplands, was bankrolled by London Records and saw him back new music by Paul Quinn, Win and James King & the Lonewolves. A largely unsuccessful reactivation of Postcard Records was attempted in the 1990s.

By the 1980s punk's DIY promise had been fulfilled as beginner labels surfaced all over the UK. Taking his influence from Postcard Records, Fast Product, Rough Trade, among others, Glaswegian Alan McGee brought his ideas to London and established the future powerhouse, Creation. From small beginnings it would soon grab the headlines with the first Jesus and Mary Chain single, and eventually become home to Teenage Fanclub, Super Furry Animals, Primal Scream, My Bloody Valentine and Creation's major cash-cow, Oasis. McGee would dabble with another label, Elevation, funded by WEA Records, but soon concentrated on Creation before selling the whole lot to Sony. He would later re-emerge with the Poptones label and a management company in the 2000s.

Alan McGee, *c.*1997

Jeremy Sutton-Hibbert / Alamy Stock Photo

Back home 53rd & 3rd Records, named after a Ramones song, was being run by Stephen Pastel, Sandy Mclean, and David Keegan of the Shop Assistants. In their brief tenure they signed buzzsaw popsters The Vaselines, BMX Bandits and The Beat Poets before calling it quits. Edinburgh retailer Avalanche Records set up its own imprint and reissued 53rd & 3rd compilations as well as new releases by the Shop Assistants, Jesse Garon and the Desperadoes, and others. Mention should also go to short-lived indie Rational Records with releases by The Delmontes and Visitors.

Rather than a slowing of pace, Scotland in the '90s brought an even more diverse range of genres to the table. Human Condition Records operated out of Chamber Recording Studios in Granton, Edinburgh – its largely grunge-driven sound famously giving Idlewild their first foray into vinyl. West coast, post-punk 'avant provocateur' Douglas MacIntyre created the Creeping Bent Organisation as an outlet for fine records by The Leopards, The Secret Goldfish, The Nectarine No. 9, as well as Alan Vega of Suicide. Even the music business students at Stow College (now part of Glasgow Kelvin College) were given the opportunity to run Electric Honey Records, under the watchful eye of Alan Rankine of The Associates. This label would let loose Belle & Sebastian's debut *Tigermilk* album, before helping bands like Snow Patrol and Biffy Clyro on their way.

The expanding dance and electronica scene was also given solid support by the Glasgow Underground label. It created an extensive house catalogue and offshoot label Breastfed Records, which produced the bonafide smash hit *Destroy Rock'n'Roll* by Isle of Skye producer Mylo. Hook Records in Aberdeen similarly enjoyed underground glory, but it was the pioneering Soma Quality Recordings in Glasgow that would enjoy real longevity. Kicked off in 1991 by Glenn Gibbons, Dave Clarke and the DJs Stuart McMillan and Orde Meikle, Soma would famously release *Da Funk* by Daft Punk, as well as bangers by Slam, Funk D'Void, Silicone Soul and hundreds of releases thereafter. Still alive and kicking in the techno world today, Soma is both a cottage industry and an international success.

Alongside sterling work from Shoeshine, Lithium, Mint and SL Records – who would unearth the John Peel favourites, Ballboy – Chemikal Underground were, for good reason, the indie buzz label of the '90s and 2000s in Scotland. These university friends and Delgados' bandmates unwittingly started something important in 1994, with a prolific inventory of band releases by Mogwai, Arab Strap, Bis, Aereogramme, Interpol, The Phantom, and others. Amid rapid-fire digital developments that have not necessarily been kind to the label, Chemikal Underground is still very much in existence, now based out of the much-admired recording studio Chem 19.

As the new millennium crept into view, the startling arrival of the internet had a colossal effect on the music industry. Some found it hard to adapt as sales of stock declined and previous business models were rendered extinct – it was sink or swim. But the internet also delivered massive opportunities. The ultimate age of DIY had arrived. Any individual with vision and ambition, plus a decent computer and connection, could broadcast themselves or set up a digital record company. Scottish labels could use the web to sell digital music, or as a portal for news, updates and physical releases. These days it is possible to create global niche audiences for the most outlandish or outsider music *and* keep up-to-date with these communities.

Ever the bastion of independence, Mogwai set up their own label early on, with Rock Action Records (called after The Stooges' drummer, Scott Asheton). Ostensibly a way of releasing music by their friends, it has morphed into a force to be reckoned with, releasing records by Part Chimp, Envy, Errors, Sacred Paws and Out Lines. Since 2010, as the operation has gained greater reach, Mogwai has funnelled its own releases across the UK and Europe through the label.

Another individual walking his own path is Keith McIvor or 'JD Twitch'. His DJ selection skills under the 'Pure' and 'Optimo' banners have inspired reverence for nearly three decades, and it was a natural progression to cut some of that good taste on vinyl. First with Oscarr and then with Optimo Music, JD Twitch unleashed an eclectic assortment of strange music into the world, including electronic, ambient and Afrobeat from the likes of Chris Carter, Happy Meals and Golden Teacher.

Fence Records was set up by Kenny Anderson in St Andrews, Fife, as a means to promote his own music and that of his brothers. Though not the most visibly lucrative venture of the '90s and 2000s, it has possibly become the most influential in more recent times. Unlikely as it may seem, Anderson's low-fidelity, self-made CD releases captured the imagination of music-lovers craving honest creativity and none

of the music biz baggage. As King Creosote, alongside his brothers Lone Pigeon and Pip Dylan, his handcrafted, anti-corporate, homespun outpourings showed a new way to approach a DIY label with zero fuss. Soon others gravitated towards the project and under the Fence Collective umbrella the label would release vinyl, compact discs and, most importantly, host mini-festivals from their home in the East Neuk of Fife, proving how the internet could actually serve small communities far away from the big cities. Fence, however, became a bit too successful for Anderson and he split with his co-conspirator Johnny Lynch (known as The Pictish Trail). Johnny Lynch has since created his own label Lost Map on the Isle of Eigg, and Fence Records has recently been releasing CDs once again as a micro-indie under Kenny Anderson's singular guidance.

Taking inspiration from many of the aforementioned, the newest breed of indie labels sees Song by Toad, Olive Grove, Last Night From Glasgow, Scottish Fiction and Triassic Tusk all vying for our attention. Their physical and digital schedules inject sparking new life into the local scene, taking it international when possible.

Compact discs, a portable storage medium
designed to record, store and play-back
audio or video data in digital form

Cabrerafoto / Shutterstock.com

Not all Scottish-friendly labels are homegrown, of course. International support for Scottish artists has come from a cross-section of major record companies and many other independents along the way. The Domino Recording Company has a close relationship with Scotland, seeing many of the country's most significant artists of the last thirty years make their way on their roster – say hello to Franz Ferdinand, King Creosote, Steve Mason and James Yorkston. Domino has even given The Pastels their own imprint, Geographic, for releases by Future Pilot AKA, Bill Wells Trio, Teenage Fanclub, and others. German outlet Marina Records has also had a love-affair with all things Glasgow indie and post-punk, releasing records by The Bathers, Paul Quinn and The Pearlfishers. Fatcat Recordings of Brighton should also invest in an office north of the border. In the last ten years they have issued an astonishing parade of The Twilight Sad, Frightened Rabbit, We Were Promised Jetpacks, Honeyblood, Paws and C Duncan to a worldwide indie guitar-loving audience.

Warp Records of Sheffield must be seen as the coolest electronica label today. It now employs Dominic Flanagan as an A&R man, thanks to his work in setting up the future-facing LuckyMe label in Edinburgh. Their biggest export, Glasgow producer Hudson Mohawke (Hudmo), has released through the label, alongside LuckyMe cohort Rustie, and is now signed up to Kanye West's own label G.O.O.D Music. Scotland now sits at the top table with the biggest names in hip hop and pop. In addition, another Glasgow electronica label, NMBRS, is also slowly growing into one of the hippest electro and house stables on the planet.

Watching and listening as a broadcaster and journalist, I wonder if this forward momentum will ever slow, if Scotland might one day cease to be quite as creative or prolific. That day hasn't yet arrived. It seems as if the Scots have an insatiable appetite for new music, whether pressed on a thin piece of vinyl, recorded on cassette, burned onto a compact disc or downloaded via digital streaming platforms. Fans love the artists that produce the music, the companies that distribute the product, and the emporiums where we can browse and buy. It's all 'Treasure'.

Opposite: Compact Audio Cassettes (CAC) referred to as music cassette tapes

FabrikaSimf / Shutterstock.com

Chapter four

Big gold dream

Britain was in a state of stagnation. The grim, grey backdrop of industrial decline, strikes, dole queues, discontent and the three-day working week was reflected in the drab music and mediocre culture of the mid- to late 1970s. Disposable pop, bland disco, directionless prog, worthy folk and smooth mainstream rock were staples, while cheesy and vulgar television programmes were an unfortunate nightly occurrence. The vast gorge between the rock élites and the record-buying youth had never been wider. Even the brief excitement generated by glam rock had evaporated, with its stars seeming tired and bloated. David Bowie was still making interesting records, the New York Dolls were turning heads, and The Sensational Alex Harvey Band had shaken things up a bit. But on the whole, music felt pedestrian to teenagers and young adults, anyone who genuinely wanted a new pop thrill. Change was needed, and change was on its way.

The term 'punk' was coined in New York and initially referred to a new collection of disparate groups emerging from the rat-infested Bowery area of the city. Ramones, Talking Heads, Blondie and Television plundered the past, lived in the moment and looked to the future. Suddenly technique wasn't everything – attitude, style and ideas were more important. Being impoverished outcasts of society was harnessed as art or worn as a badge of honour. Those on the New York scene, with their ripped jeans and second-hand leathers, air of defiance and detachment, ignited and inspired similar malcontents in London. The Damned, Sex Pistols, The Clash and others rose from the gutters to send shockwaves through the music industry, youth culture and old-guard alike. Like skiffle and '50s rock'n'roll all over again, punk was the epitome of DIY and spread like wildfire across the country. With Manchester pogo-ing and Liverpool gobbing, Scotland soon joined the fray – though as you might expect, the response north of the border was nuanced and unique.

Though Glasgow, with the largest population mass, had been more productive and discerning about rock'n'roll during the '60s and '70s, it was Edinburgh that first took the raw, rampaging rhythms of punk to its bosom. After the shocking Sex Pistols

Pages 50–51: Punks at a rock festival in
Kelvingrove Park, Glasgow, 1978

'Bill Grundy' television appearance and a so-called riot at a Stranglers gig in the City Halls, the Lord Provost famously commented that there were enough hooligans in Glasgow without importing them from down south, and punk rock found itself banned. Johnny Rotten may have hooted with delight, but the city's scene was momentarily thwarted. Young punks had to travel to The Silver Thread Hotel at nearby Paisley, or head far east to the Nite Club or Tiffany's in Edinburgh, to see their safety-pinned heroes throw shapes and incite a little teenage insurrection.

While Glasgow remained ensconced in double-denim and hard-rockin' blues bands, in far-off Australia the band AC/DC, perhaps the greatest distillation of heavy rock'n'roll yet, were on an upward trajectory. Beginning in 1973 they would go on to become one of the biggest selling rock bands in history. A mirror image of punk in many ways, they played back-to-basics, raw rock'n'roll using minimal chord progressions, but with energy and aggression. Perhaps un-hip if compared to the

AC/DC performing in New York City, 1984

Ramones, they were aesthetically similar. Although founded in Australia, the main focus of the band, Bon Scott, and guitarists Angus and Malcolm Young, were born and bred in Scotland, leaving for Down Under in 1963. But it wasn't long before they were welcomed into the hearts, minds and souls of Scottish rock fans. Indeed the country now dubiously claims AC/DC as its own, whether Australia likes it or not. Their album *If You Want Blood, You've Got It ...* is one of the greatest live rock'n'roll recordings ever, chronicled in front of a rabid fanbase at the Glasgow Apollo in 1978. Their career soon became a template for all future rockers over an astonishing five-decade lifespan and fifteen studio albums. Tragically Bon Scott died in 1980, but the Young brothers continue to play and have never forgotten their Scottish roots.

Although punk was regarded as a complete 'year zero' by some, it was actually quite reverent to certain, selective areas of rock'n'roll history. Most punk bands admired the beat and mod scenes of the '60s and the short sharp shock of the '50s. None more so than Edinburgh art-rockers The Rezillos. Forming at the Edinburgh College of Art in 1976, they threw together the bits they liked from the recent past – Joe Meek, girl-groups, rockabilly – and sped things up by adding PVC, wrap-around sunglasses, quiffed hair and a Sci-Fi shtick. They were an exhilarating blast of colour and soon had oddball pop songs to back up their onstage riot. Local DJ, manager and club promoter Lenny Love took them in hand and set up arguably Scotland's first independent punk label, Sensible Records. The Rezillos' debut single *Can't Stand My Baby* was released and immediately blew up, with influential Radio 1 DJ John Peel loving the song. After performing in London the group was snapped up by Stateside label SIRE, home to Blondie and the Ramones. However, for the fabulously named members of the Rezillos – Fay Fife, Luke Warm, William Mysterious, Gayle Warning, Sci-Fi Harris, Angel Paterson, Simon Templar, Eugene Reynolds, and so on – the band's lifespan would be short and sweet, despite hitting the charts and the eponymous television show with their anthem *Top Of The Pops*.

After a joyous first album *Can't Stand The Rezillos*, divisions and musical differences put paid to the band and they split in 1979. Though the group would return in a slightly altered guise as The Revillos, achieving a cult following for a string of eccentric and fun releases, their promise was never fully realised. Guitarist and songwriter Jo Callis (a.k.a. Luke Warm) would go on to play with post-punks Shake and funk-punks Boots for Dancing. Callis eventually joined The Human League and wrote much of their smash-hit album *Dare*, including the number-one single *Don't You Want Me?*

Other Edinburgh bands giving it a go included The Valves, who had three retro-influenced singles and lasted from 1977–79, building up a strong homegrown following thanks to snappy, punk-pop tunes *For Adolfs' Only* and *There Ain't No Surf In Portobello*. The Prats were a school band that ended in 1981 when, well, they left school. With an extended-play record and two singles of discordant, primitive, playful punk, they won praise from John Peel before they disappeared. The Prats were re-evaluated after their song *General Davis* was extraordinarily featured in the Hollywood film 'The Manchurian Candidate' (2004). The Questions, also from Edinburgh, signed to Zoom in 1978 while still at school. Paul Weller took them under his wing in 1980 and they supported The Jam on tour. Although an album was released, their initial promise was never quite fulfilled. The Rezillos, The Valves and Boots for Dancing all re-formed in the late 2000s, once again winning over Edinburgh's post-punk hearts.

Another Pretty Face had potential but were also short-lived. Mike Scott formed the band in Edinburgh while at university and writing the *Jungleland* fanzine. With inspiration from new firebrands The Clash, as well as the more considered Patti Smith and Bruce Springsteen, his bohemian songwriting nous was on display almost from the off. Debut single *All The Boys Love Carrie* (1979) was acclaimed by the music press

The Rezillos, *c.*1970s

peteranderson.photos

and the band was duly signed to Virgin Records in 1980. A first album was unfortunately shelved and the band were set to quit Virgin to release music on Scott's own Chicken Jazz label. With a name change to Funhouse bringing no greater interest, however, the group folded and Scott went on to achieve cult status and major chart success with The Waterboys.

Fife was early to the punk party too. After the success of rockers Nazareth, Dunfermline youth perhaps sensed their generation could have a crack. The Skids paired the exuberant and somewhat naive frontman Richard 'Curly' Jobson with the chiming guitars and songwriting suss of Stuart Adamson, soon to be one of the country's genuine guitar heroes. A debut extended player or EP was financed by a local record shop and Fife's first punk band set to work, gigging enthusiastically up and down the land before decamping to London for a while. Building a grassroots crowd and yet more radio support from avid punk supporter John Peel, the band

The Skids, (left to right) Stuart Adamson,
William Simpson, Tom Kellichan and
Richard Jobson, Edinburgh, February 1978

were soon signed to Virgin Records in 1978 and scored a top-twenty album *Scared To Dance*, featuring the top-ten and best-known song *Into The Valley* (1979). More hits followed and three more albums, including their most successful *The Absolute Game* which hit the top ten. But despite their increasingly polished, new-wave sound, Adamson's visionary guitar work, Jobson's chiselled good looks and boundless onstage energy, the band dissolved in 1982, with fourth and final album *Joy*, from an entirely different line-up, seen as a disappointment. Stuart Adamson would go on to form the hugely successful Big Country, with Richard Jobson singing briefly in another group, The Armoury Show, before launching a career as a model, actor, poet and filmmaker.

In their hey-day The Skids were a force to be reckoned with and massively popular, blending boot-boy, football terrace bravado with an inquisitive intellect and anthemic melodies. The band has re-formed twice – in 2007 to celebrate their thirtieth anniversary and the life of Stuart Adamson who died in 2001, and again in 2017 to mark their fortieth. Fans lapped it up on both occasions.

Central to the success and proliferation of punk and new wave was the independent fanzine and label culture that exploded alongside the music itself. These labels had sprung up around the UK, and globally, as a street-wise reaction to the safe decision-making and studied investment of major record companies. In Edinburgh alone there were the labels Sensible, Fast Product, Pop : Aural, and Zoom which was set up and run by Bruce Findlay the record-shop boss and later music industry mogul and manager. Findlay would soon look west to find the band that would change his, and indeed Scotland's, musical life.

Although further underground, thanks to the aforementioned comments by the Lord Provost, Glasgow's punk scene was also in full flight. The Jolt, The Back Stabbers (including the magnificently named lead singer Rev Volting) and Johnny & the Self Abusers all crawled out of the woodwork to play pubs and biker bars where possible. Apart from their truly tremendous punk band name, the Self Abusers signed to pub rock label Chiswick Records for a solitary single, *Saints and Sinners,* before splitting on the day of release. The two groups that rose from the ashes were The Cuban Heels and a certain Simple Minds, featuring Jim Kerr and Charlie Burchill.

A startlingly modern group from the very start, Simple Minds steered clear of the basic buzzsaw attack of generic punk and looked to Bowie, Roxy Music and Kraftwerk as muses. Guitars were in the mix, but so were synthesisers. Punk rock may have blown open the doors to their creativity, but they were now free to pioneer new sounds and aesthetics. Gone were the safety-pins and torn jeans in favour of eye-liner, bowl-cuts, grandad shirts and charity-shop suits. They were most definitely post-punk and proud. Bruce Findlay courted the band and became their manager and label boss, with Zoom taking investment from major label cohorts at Arista. A rather disappointing debut album *Life In A Day* was produced, followed by a more experi-mental second set *Real To Real Cacophony*, both in 1979. Although the band's full potential had not yet been realised, their ambition was already on show. By the time the third album *Empires and Dance* was delivered, Simple Minds were making serious headway. The widescreen vocals and shimmering guitars were now backed by a more robust funk-influenced rhythm section and an overt love of German *kosmische* music (also known as 'krautrock'). *I Travel* became their first great single

Simple Minds, (left to right) Mel Gaynor,
Charlie Burchill, Derek Forbes, Jim Kerr
and Mick MacNeil, 1984

Trinity Mirror / Mirrorpix / Alamy Stock
Photo

and pointed forwards. In 1981 Simple Minds signed to Virgin Records, releasing their finest collection yet as *Sons And Fascination / Sister Feelings Call* – with a genuine hit in *Love Song* – more evidence of their motoric, repetitive beat obsessions. It was apparent that the band could transcend their underground roots and break into the mainstream at any time – but when? The answer would lie in the years directly ahead.

In Edinburgh a collection of acts was loosely creating their own scene around the Fast Product and Pop:Aural labels, masterminded by entrepreneur Bob Last and his partner Hilary Morrison. Their initial view of Fast was as some kind of production house that might not even include music. Ideas were as much about the aesthetics, design and marketing as about the music itself. Inspired by the Buzzcocks' *Spiral Scratch* EP, regarded as the first truly independent and self-financed punk release, Fast put out a slew of groundbreaking non-Scottish acts such as The Mekons, Gang of Four, The Human League and the Dead Kennedys from San Francisco. The label was one of the few guiding lights of the UK punk scene, influencing all around them. Perhaps Scotland's post-punk eureka moment was the release of the astonishing single *Adultery / Horrorshow* by Edinburgh's Scars. It set the bar high and showed Scots could make extremely original and fresh-sounding new music with no apparent influence or help from London. Their visceral sound and sense of confidence would permeate through their contemporaries, their Glasgow peers, and younger bands in waiting.

The Scars' original sound came from the interplay between Paul Research's exquisite, spiralling guitar lines and singer Robert King's provocative and often garbled singing style. Their debut single may have been a shot in the arm for Scotland's scene by 1979, but the release of their first album *Author! Author!* over two years later led to faint praise because of its more polished new-wave feel. Although asked to perform two John Peel Radio 1 sessions and appear on the 'Old Grey Whistle Test', their slightly confused new-romantic image and erratic release schedule eroded ambition and the band fell apart. Throw in some feisty characters and a touch of infighting, and they were history by 1982.

Fast forward over twenty years and 'sampledelic', electronica duo Lemon Jelly decided to use a section of the Scar's *Horrorshow* on their single *The Shouty Track*,

reviving some interest in the band in 2005. Scars then re-formed in December 2010 for an incendiary live show at Edinburgh's Picture House. Yet again this was a band that never quite realised its potential, though on further investigation *Author! Author!* is still an inventive work and a rewarding listen.

Fellow agitators in the capital included a combo formed from the vestiges of local punks The Dirty Reds. Inspired by The Slits and Subway Sect, and the primitive and confrontational opening acts on The Clash's 'White Riot' tour, the Fire Engines were named after a 13th Floor Elevators song and led by the inimitable Davy Henderson. They are now regarded as hugely influential on countless independent guitar bands that have followed in their wake. Opting for a jagged, discordant sound with high-treble, single-note guitar lines and clattering drums, Henderson's wordplay and ear for a pop-hook marked them out. With their infamous fifteen- or twenty-minute live sets, they were natural successors to punk with a belligerent attitude, a post-modern anti-consumerist vision, and a love of Captain Beefheart and James Chance. Debut single *Get Up And Use Me* effortlessly grabbed the attention of the UK's discerning music press, and Bob Last's new label Pop:Aural took them on, issuing a mini album and two excellent singles in *Candyskin* and *Big Gold Dream*. Like their thrashy and abrasive live shows, however, the band were not destined or designed to last; yet their legacy lives on through acts they have influenced, as well as Davy Henderson's excellent subsequent groups Win, The Nectarine No. 9, and Sexual Objects. Although commercial remuneration may not have come his way, Henderson is one of the true unsung heroes of Scottish rock'n'roll.

Perhaps the most acclaimed Edinburgh group of this loose, late '70s scene was

Davy Henderson of the Fire Engines

© Harry Papadopoulos, courtesy Street Level Photoworks

Josef K, a Kafka-inspired and deliberately obstinate quartet originally known as TV Art. Dressed in dark suits, unsmiling, with a perpetual sense of impending doom, the combination of singer Paul Haig's anti-rock stance and delivery with Malcolm Ross's scratchy jangly guitar lines was a serious soundtrack to grim, grey Britain. Unsurprisingly Paul Morley, the pop conceptualist and individual who helped to discover Joy Division, was a huge champion from their first single *Chance Meeting* on the Absolute label. Hooking up with the fledgling Postcard Records, on the insistence of Orange Juice's Stephen Daly, they dug out a brittle and uncompromising furrow. Once again here was a band that set an indie blueprint for future generations, but produced few returns at the time. Following acclaimed single releases, they abandoned their debut album *Sorry For Laughing* on account of its sterile, bland production, scuppering its release. They then connected with a Belgian label Les Disques du Crépiscule and re-recorded many of the songs for their now debut album *The Only Fun In Town*. A jagged, hi-energy, punk-funk document of the band's wiry sound, it met with a middling critical reception, seeing the band disintegrate by

Josef K

© Harry Papadopoulos, courtesy Street Level Photoworks

1982. Haig went on to have an erratic solo career, with Ross joining Orange Juice and Aztec Camera in the near future. Massively influential and well-loved, Josef K's rightful reputation as post-punk forerunners now survives their short existence. Bravely, they have never seen fit to re-form.

'The Sound of Young Scotland' was a slogan heralded by mythmaker Alan Horne, who alongside Stephen Daly built up a short-lived mini-empire in 1979 from a cupboard in the West End of Glasgow. Postcard Records signed bands such as Josef K, Australian songsmiths The Go-Betweens and the precocious young talent Aztec Camera, but the label was mainly a vehicle for its prodigies The Nu-Sonics. Formed in the distinctly middle-class Glasgow suburb of Bearsden in 1976, the band's name was changed to Orange Juice in 1979. Fronted by the boyish, be-fringed (soon to be be-quiffed) Edwyn Collins, here was a band that took the DIY ethic of punk, jangle of The Byrds, thump of '60s soul and the pop-art cool of The Velvet Underground as its own to create an anti-macho, joyful and somewhat primitive form of new pop. Horne was obsessed with the sound and soon the London music press was similarly impressed, especially by the label's impudent media releases and their tongue-in-cheek marketing ideas. Some in Glasgow considered Postcard Records arrogant and a touch élitist, but Horne, Daly and Collins were all admirers of the avant-garde artist Andy Warhol, impresario Malcolm McLaren and the '60s Situationists. They had similar aspirations and wanted to make their own mark – though on a shoestring budget.

Postcard Records would put out just twelve singles, and only one album release (Josef K), with new signings The Bluebells and The Jazzateers waiting in the wings. The label could have gone on to bigger and better things, establishing itself as a northern indie powerhouse, but some things aren't meant to be. Its lasting heritage and influence have been widely documented over the past thirty-five years, but the excellent music and brass-neck of the young Glasgow chancers is now legendary. Orange Juice, of course, outlasted the label, with Horne acting as an A&R person for the band. They recorded a John Peel session and signed to Polydor, releasing four albums and scoring a number-eight single with *Rip It Up*. Their musical, graphic and conceptual vision has touched almost every generation of Glasgow music since, and

by the band's end in 1984/85 Edwyn Collins had only just started. His solo career would reap greater rewards in the 1990s and beyond.

After a couple of underground flourishes on two solo albums for the Demon label, his third, *Gorgeous George*, would skyrocket with the surprise hit of lead single *A Girl Like You*, recorded in his own self-built London-based studio. Although both single and album would go top ten in the UK, the song would also take Collins around the world on a seemingly never-ending promotional tour as it sold and sold and sold. Unfortunately subsequent records would never quite achieve the same glorious heights. Two more albums followed in the '90s and 2000s, before tragedy struck. In 2005, out of nowhere, Collins suffered two catastrophic brain haemorrhages, resulting in some one-sided physical paralysis and aphasia, where he was unable to formulate speech in the way he once had.

After months of physical, mental and vocal rehabilitation, Collins astonishingly managed to resume his music career against all the odds. His mind was absolutely fine and a new sense of optimism and joy had grabbed him. Discovering that he could

Orange Juice, with Edwyn Collins

© Harry Papadopoulos, courtesy Street Level Photoworks

sing fluently, while his speech was still staggered and stumbling, he embarked on recording and playing live as soon as possible. Since 2007 he has released three more superb albums and a selection of singles, as well as playing shows throughout the UK and the USA. With his wife Grace Maxwell by his side, he runs his own label AED (Analogue Enhance Digital), has collaborated with artists such as Roddy Frame, Franz Ferdinand and The Cribs, and continues to produce a range of other artists. Recently he and Grace have moved their studio and home to the Highlands, where his recovery and musical work continues. With his music and a love of drawing and illustration, art has been the great healer for Edwyn Collins. It is an extraordinary story.

Although Glasgow's punk ban was lifted, the scene was fragmented and hard to contain. But there were some mainstay characters. Clare Grogan was a regular at gigs in Glasgow, Edinburgh and Paisley, attending concerts as a teenager. While filming the soon-to-be-mythic Bill Forsyth film 'Gregory's Girl', she joined school friends in a new-wave act called Altered Images. After contacting their heroes Siouxsie and the Banshees, the band, unbelievably, were invited to tour with the Banshees, conveniently opening the door to a genuine career. Quickly signed to CBS Records, Altered Images gained the support of John Peel and recorded a single with Banshees' Steve Severin. A debut album was quickly made with venerated producer Martin Rushent at the helm and veritable pop classic *Happy Birthday* went to number three. Altered Images could do no wrong, with their well-known actress/lead singer, guitars, synths and bucket-loads of perfect pop at their disposal. More sure-fire hits followed – *I Could Be Happy* and *Don't Talk To Me About Love* – but the albums *Pinky Blue* and *Bite* disappointed band members and fans alike, with fractures in the band beginning to appear. On the eve of an American tour, possibly Scotland's most successful, chart-friendly, new-wave act yet had fallen by the wayside – mainly down to youthful inexperience and the harsh expectations of the music industry.

Grogan has remained in the creative business as a presenter and actor on radio and television, and as an author of books for children. She also performs Altered Images' hits onstage at '80s-themed festivals throughout the UK. Johnny McElhone from the band would soon reappear in successful '80s acts Hipsway and Texas, while

Steven Lironi would marry Grogan and become a record producer, label boss and restaurateur. All was not lost.

Other punk scenesters, and Nu-Sonics/Orange Juice devotees, who would soon go on to hit pop gold were Strawberry Switchblade. Named after a song by Orange Juice's James Kirk, duo Jill Bryson and Rose McDowall sported an audacious post-punk look of back-combed hair, polka-dots and liberal use of eye-liner, that secured immediate attention. Initially they had a full band and, with the ubiquitous support of John Peel, managed to connect with fellow Scot and music manager Bill Drummond, later of electronic band The KLF. With friends and associates, he set them up with a small label deal and released debut single *Trees and Flowers*, selling thousands of copies in independent shops across Britain. The band was ditched at the behest of a larger label, however, and they became a synth-pop sensation with their song *Since Yesterday* hitting number five in 1985. More singles and a decent album followed, but by 1986 Bryson and McDowall had split. Some original demos

Altered Images, with Clare Grogan, 1980s

Pictorial Press Ltd / Alamy Stock Photo

Strawberry Switchblade, Rose McDowall (left) and Jill Bryson (right), 1985

Pictorial Press Ltd / Alamy Stock Photo

have appeared recently and both women have continued to make music, with McDowall the more prolific.

Simple Minds, Altered Images and Strawberry Switchblade were only three acts to make use of synthesisers. As myriad new varieties hit music retailers across the land, with prices falling and technology improving by the day, they became the every-man, every-band sort of instrument. Anyone could make music with a reasonably user-friendly synthesiser – perhaps punk's DIY promise had finally come to fruition in post-punk and synth-pop.

Bronski Beat, featuring the high-pitched Scottish soul-man Jimmy Somerville, stormed the charts with their openly gay and proud anthem *Smalltown Boy* from the debut album *The Age of Consent* (1984). Annie Lennox and Dave Stewart, meanwhile, had risen from the remnants of The Tourists in 1980 to create the Eurythmics. Somerville would soon go on to form The Communards and top the charts; Lennox and Stewart's Eurythmics would become one of the biggest bands on the planet. Another duo with an incredible singer, Billy Mackenzie, alongside cohort Alan Rankine, would neatly bridge post-punk inventiveness and the vertical ambition of the advancing '80s – The Associates.

Mackenzie was a Dundee lad, and would remain so until his untimely death in 1997. But it was in Edinburgh that he met Rankine, the two working to earn quick cash singing cabaret songs in hotels. Effortlessly penning their own material from 1976 onwards, Mackenzie and Rankine stopped the club work and officially became The Associates in 1979, forging their own distinctive careers.

The opening salvo was an unauthorised cover of Bowie's *Boys Keep Swinging*,

Bronski Beat, with Jimmy Somerville (centre)

peteranderson.photos

that amazingly attracted the attention of Fiction Records. From there they developed a sound quite unlike anyone else. Rankine was the guitarist, multi-instrumentalist and musical leader in some ways, while the sartorially impressive Mackenzie, with his freewheeling, operatic and utterly wild vocal style, made the duo stand out a mile. Although not a definitive synth-pop band, the genre worked in The Associates' favour. By their second studio work *Sulk* they had hit the top ten of the album charts and scored a number-nine single with the staggering *Party Fears Two* – a song that sounds just as luscious and outlandish now as the day it was released.

American giant Sire Records approached the group, but Mackenzie turned them down. Rankine then left and commercial fortunes declined, as Mackenzie continued under the band name until 1990. Despite this, the astonishing music they made, and their brief moment in the spotlight, would go on to enchant listeners for generations to come. Of course, some of the ludicrous behind-the-scenes stories about The

Annie Lennox in Edinburgh, 1987

Associates were equally celebrated. Mackenzie, it is said, fed his beloved whippets smoked salmon on the record company tab; and on finally being released from his record deal he asked for one last taxi home – from London to Dundee!

Post-punk manifested itself in all sorts of places. The unlikely location of Ellon in the north east spawned a group more in tune with New York than neighbouring Aberdeen. Mirroring the sounds of Liquid Liquid and ESG, APB's punk-funk found favour with local label Oily Records who released the first flush of material. John Peel's support followed, as did that of 'The Big Apple' itself. Apparently APB singles were being spun to dance-floors across the city's clubs and so began a love-affair with New York. APB made twelve visits to record there and open for acts like The Clash and James Brown. They would headline infamous spots such as The Ritz and Irving Plaza, hear their music on local radio rotation and be generally embraced by the city's underground. Their recorded output stretches roughly from 1981–88, but the band re-formed in 2006 to reignite the funk for some live shows and recordings.

By now synths may have been the dominant sound and the polished stadium rock of the 1980s was just around the corner, but the embers of down'n'dirty punk

The Associates, Billy Mackenzie (left) and
Alan Rankine (right)

© Harry Papadopoulos, courtesy Street
Level Photoworks

rock were still burning. Although punk had initially been regarded as a working-class phenomenon, it had actually been saturated by middle-class kids and art-school drop-outs. Some wanted to take it to the housing schemes across the land and reflect what they saw as real working-class rage.

By the early 1980s a new street-punk had surfaced – 'Oi!' and then 'UK82'. It was hard, fast and angry with no subtlety whatsoever. Many of the original punks hated it, but it soon spread across the country. Perhaps the most successful, certainly the longest lasting, of these groups came from Edinburgh. The Exploited formed in 1979 and rose to prominence with ex-squaddie Wattie Buchan on lead shouting and John Duncan ('Big' John Duncan) on guitar. Bassist Gary McCormack had been in Josef K briefly and would reinvent himself as an actor in the 1990s and 2000s. Their debut album *Punks Not Dead* was a call to arms that went top twenty in 1981 and is still widely regarded in the genre. The band built a dedicated following, famously appearing on 'Top of the Pops' in full Mohican punk regalia to play *Dead Cities*, and have continued to conquer the underground worlds of hardcore punk and cross-over thrash, adored by anti-establishment, chicken-headed, pogo-fanatics to this day. Although never critically acclaimed, their influence has stretched far further than most bands from this small country.

Mirroring the political changes in society from the late '70s to the early '80s, a cultural bomb had gone off and pop music was changed forever. The punks had booted out the hippies and prog rockers and a new well of creativity had sprung forth with Scotland pioneering various new genres. These were exciting times and the shake-up had churned out huge amounts of interesting and inventive music. But in terms of commerciality and reach, its greatest achievements were waiting on the horizon. Scottish pop was about to come of age and go global.

Chapter five
Glittering prize

Under the Conservative prime minister Margaret Thatcher, the 1980s saw the biggest political shake-up in the United Kingdom since the Second World War. Nationalised industries were privatised at an unwavering pace, with a new set of deregulated free markets encouraged. Scotland watched its primary mining and steel industries almost disappear, and working-class communities moved to adapt quickly to a new type of economic thinking. Trade unions became less powerful, the state shrank, unemployment rose and the fiscal landscape changed irreparably. At the same time, the costs of developing and extracting oil from the North Sea had become more economical and the rewards would soon be pumped into the ailing UK economy, along with the spoils of privatisation. Soon the political battle-lines were drawn. Scotland, though socially conservative, was a left-leaning country with a majority voting Labour since the 1950s.

Musicians were some of the first to take sides and soon an activism not witnessed since the 1960s appeared. This time, however, rather than grubby denims and flares, the look and sound on the street began to sharpen up. Art reflected both sides of the divide – the dispossessed on one side, the aspirational and ambitious on the other.

The 1980s may be portrayed as all designer suits, hair gel, yachts and expense accounts, but there were many different sides to this decade and music would reflect them all. Pop had already undergone many changes in its relatively short life, but after the shattering impact of punk it was now free to be whatever it wanted to be. Technology was a driving influence too, and as studio equipment and techniques were updated so was the sound of the music. Keyboards, synthesisers, electronics and computers were heard more frequently alongside traditional guitars. The growing record-buying, gig-going public presented a far greater platform – and business was key. Sales, marketing, advertising and image now seemed more important than ever.

Despite the oncoming ostentation of the '80s, songwriting and storytelling were

Pages 70–71: Crowds at the Live Aid
concert, Wembley Stadium, London,
13 July 1985

© Trinity Mirror / Mirrorpix / Alamy Stock
Photo

still at the heart of everything Scotland did. Soon more traditional, lilting melodies and themes would be heard in pop. Traces of Glasgow, Edinburgh or Dundee accents had been heard occasionally in the past, but the music was fairly homogenous. Whatever political bent, there was now an ambition from some to have their national voice heard and to represent the country's identity. For perhaps the first time, aside from sporadic tartan-clad novelty songs, Scottish pop was visibly and audibly ready to assert itself upon the ever-changing musical map.

London remained a major pull for dedicated musicians. Those most committed to their art made the move, for better or worse. Annie Lennox, who has become one of Scotland's most famous voices, did exactly that. With her distinct and well-defined Aberdonian accent and obvious musical prowess, she relocated to London to study at the Royal Academy of Music. Soon disillusioned by college, she met Peter 'Peet' Coombes and Dave Stewart and joined The Catch which was swiftly renamed The Tourists. Three albums and a raft of singles followed, reaching the top ten twice, though the band was never particularly lauded by the critics. They also toured with Roxy Music and appeared on BBC's 'The Old Grey Whistle Test'. A strong start, but not quite the big time. After the band parted ways in 1980, Lennox and Stewart, a couple up to that point, continued to write as a duo and to plan a new project.

Eurythmics may have had a shaky start in 1981 with their debut Conny Plank produced album *In The Garden* issued to only slight applause, but their time was nigh. At home in London they made use of a bank loan to design their own small makeshift studio with new portable synthesisers and a more electronic outlook. With no one watching the clock, they had time to experiment and make the music they wanted. The results changed their careers spectacularly. The album's title track *Sweet Dreams (Are Made Of This)* spawned a massive single, hitting the number-two spot in the UK and topping the US charts. Followed by another hit *Love Is A Stranger*, the duo exploded across the international pop scene and Lennox became a star over-night. With her dyed-orange crew-cut and androgynous suits, Annie from Aberdeen was a truly modern pop star with voice and charisma to match.

The duo's run of albums from then until 1990 was sensational as they became one of the biggest chart acts on the planet. The popularity of the singles grew with

every release, including *Who's That Girl?*, *Here Comes The Rain Again*, *There Must Be An Angel (Playing With My Heart)*, *Thorn In My Side* and *When Tomorrow Comes*. Each album saw the duo change stylistically, but always pen memorable tunes and expand their mass of supporters. By 1990, after eight albums in as many years, the two grew apart and put Eurythmics on hold. Lennox went on to score two number-one solo albums, with the band coming out of their hiatus to record and tour another album in 1999. Rumours abound that the duo may record again, but they both have full lives in and out of music. Annie Lennox OBE is now a political activist and philanthropist as well as songwriter. To date she has sold around 80 million albums, won eight Brit awards, four Ivor Novellos, a Golden Globe, four Grammy awards, and much more. Realistically she has to be regarded as one of the most successful Scottish artists of all time.

Cambuslang lad James 'Midge' Ure began his musical journey in Glasgow at just sixteen. In 1972 he joined a local band called Salvation. Changing the name to Slik two years later, they floated from glam-rock roots towards a smoother bubble-gum sound with the help of the Bay City Rollers' writing duo Bill Martin and Phil Coulter. Attired in American baseball shirts and led by a fresh-faced Ure, they hit the top spot in the UK singles chart with the rather saccharine *Forever And Ever* in 1976. This wouldn't be Midge Ure's last time at the top of the charts, and marked the beginning of a durable, varied and incredibly successful career. As punk and new wave ruled the waves Slik were deemed outdated, so Midge Ure moved to London in 1977 to join Glen Matlock in his post-Sex Pistols outfit, Rich Kids. Ure played rhythm

Eurythmics, Dave Stewart and Annie
Lennox, *c*.1981

guitar and sang during their short tenure and only album, but left with bandmate Rusty Egan to experiment with synthesiser sounds.

Thus began a ridiculously busy and productive period in Midge Ure's life, as part of three very different and highly successful bands – the new-romantic ensemble Visage alongside Egan; harmonising guitar rockers Thin Lizzy with friend Phil Lynott; and the re-booted art-synth quartet Ultravox who would soon go on to enjoy their greatest commercial period. The year 1980 was to prove a remark-able one for the singer/songwriter, as he pen-ned Visage's biggest single *Fade To Grey*, Phil Lynott's biggest solo record *Yellow Pearl,* and the enormous radio hit *Vienna* for Ultravox. Eventually it was Ultravox and a budding solo career that would claim priority as Ure's stock rose high on the charts. By 1981, with the launch of cable and satellite channel MTV, songs like *Vienna* and *Dancing With Tears In*

My Eyes, which were pioneering in the world of video as well as audio, would make Midge Ure one of the era's defining pop faces.

Ivor Novello awards, chart-topping solo albums and more Ultravox success followed, seeing Ure carve out an individual life as a musician. His finest hour, how-ever, came in 1984 when, assisted by The Boomtown Rats firebrand Bob Geldof, he wrote and arranged *Do They Know It's Christmas?* for a troop of contemporary megastars who gathered together under the name of 'Band Aid'. Appalled by the urgent BBC TV coverage of mass starvation and malnutrition in Ethiopia, Band Aid would instigate a global campaign that went on to raise countless millions for desperate people in their darkest hour of need. The single alone sold almost four

Ultravox, (left to right) Chris Cross, Midge Ure, Billy Currie and Warren Cann, 1984

million copies. Followed by the Live Aid concerts, it was an astonishing achievement and one for which Midge Ure OBE and all those concerned with Live Aid should feel rightly proud.

Pure pop abounded in the 1980s and Scotland's success rate was reasonably high. Fiction Factory from Perth made a memorable impression with their debut single *Feels Like Heaven* (1983) reaching number six, with radio rotation and chart positions around the globe. In the same vein, offering up a type of crooning synth-pop, were H$_2$O, the songwriting project of the Glasgow musician Ian Donaldson, who scored a number-seventeen hit single with *I Dream To Sleep* in 1983.

Glasgow-born B A Robertson managed to straddle the worlds of the novelty pop, TV-presenting, film-acting and serious song-craft around the late '70s and into the '80s. A force of nature and someone who didn't take himself too seriously, Robertson went on to attain a number of top-twenty hits including the humorous *Bang Bang*. As well as sending himself up as a guest presenter on 'Top of the Pops' and 'Friday Night, Saturday Morning', he would co-write *Carrie* and *Wired for Sound* for Cliff Richard, as well as Mike & the Mechanics' *The Living Years* which was a global smash and won an Ivor Novello award. With film acting roles, a penned World Cup song and even a two-part documentary on Scottish pop called 'Jock'n'Roll', B A Robertson was rarely out of the public eye between 1979 and 1990 but is rarely seen or heard from these days.

By 1982 the demise of Postcard Records saw a new set of groups follow in the label's footsteps. The Jazzateers recorded an entire album for the label, which was never released. They would go on to have an erratic career and multiple line-ups, including two well-loved singers Grahame 'Skin' Skinner and then Paul Quinn. The

Midge Ure performs at Live Aid, 13 July 1985

Phil Dent / Getty Images

band enjoyed success in the independent charts when briefly signed to Rough Trade, but split and re-formed too many times to retain any real impact. Ex-members then formed Bourgie Bourgie, who were signed to a major label and had two minor chart placings before their debut album was likewise shelved.

Postcard Records' Alan Horne was courted by the major world and London Records in particular, providing funds for a new label he named Swamplands. Many contemporaries from his Glasgow beginnings were signed, and a few of those he admired from the Pop:Aural label, including Davy Henderson's project Win. Eschewing the Fire Engines' abrasiveness, this new band had more in common with the polished new-pop of ABC and Heaven 17, taking conceptual post-consumerism and bombastic production to a new level. Though stuffed with melodic gold, the albums *Uh! Tears Baby* and *Freaky Trigger* did not truly connect with the audience they deserved. The single *You've Got The Power* did become an anthem for a while, thanks to the song underpinning a lager advert; but much like the rest of their material, Win's addictive subversive rush was 'chewing gum to the ears'. The irrepressible Davy Henderson would return in the '90s and 2000s with perhaps his two best groups of all, The Nectarine No. 9 and Sexual Objects.

Two immediate winners from the Postcard Records fall-out were Aztec Camera and The Bluebells. The latter saw brothers Ken and Dave McCluskey team up with Robert Hodgens, renamed Bobby Bluebell, to release on the budding Postcard label in 1981. They were well-connected already, counting Altered Images as friends and having played support to Orange Juice. Alan Horne encouraged their musical ambitions at first and, despite Postcard's demise, the band quickly hit a run of good luck, gaining support from Elvis Costello. Soon they signed to London Records. The singles *Cath*, *I'm Falling* and the joyous *Young At Heart* lodged themselves in the charts and firmly in the Scottish pop pantheon. Though originally written for bonafide pop-princesses Bananarama, *Young At Heart* went top ten for The Bluebells in 1984 when first released, but also topped the UK charts in 1993 on the back of a car advert. The band went their separate ways in 1986, but re-formed briefly in the '90s and 2000s. Stepping beyond their jangly, introspective roots, the breezy, folk-tinged melodies of The Bluebells were effortless and showed a new vision of Scottish pop

that would influence songwriters in the future. Now it was possible simultaneously to have hits and be unashamedly Scottish without seeming parochial.

The splendidly named Aztec Camera always sounded ambitious, and in central songwriter, guitarist and prodigy Roddy Frame a star was born. After meeting Edwyn Collins when Frame was just sixteen, he released two singles on the Postcard Records label in 1981. The indie world soon woke up to this precocious talent, with counter-culture stronghold label Rough Trade snapping him up. Stylish debut album *High Land, Hard Rain* was released in 1983 showcasing the mature, lovelorn songwriting and arranging skills of the teenager on excellent tracks such as *Oblivious* and *Walk Out To Winter*. Inspired by David Bowie and punk while growing up in East Kilbride, Frame set about widening his sphere of influences and life experience over a rather individual career, spending time in America, London and further globetrotting, soaking up classic Bob Dylan and Bruce Springsteen albums, hip hop, rhythm'n'blues, reggae and FM radio chart pop. Frame's music has beaten a highly singular path and appealed to a loyal, niche audience over the decades.

The Bluebells

© Harry Papadopoulos, courtesy Street Level Photoworks

Never in any kind of rush, Frame – both in Aztec Camera and as a solo artist – has worked with the Japanese polymath Ryuichi Sakamoto, Mark Knopfler of Dire Straits and Mick Jones of The Clash, among others. His sound has always remained his own, but in 1987 he stretched out to encompass the high gloss of *Somewhere In My Heart*, a number-three single from the album *Love*. It would become his biggest radio hit and continues to be a certifiable sing-along whenever it's played.

A reluctant pop star, Roddy Frame reappears from time to time with a new collection of songs, or to accompany friend Edwyn Collins on guitar. He celebrated the thirtieth anniversary of the album *Love* in 2013 with a string of shows, much to the delight of his fans.

As Scottish pop splintered, some shied away from the introverted amateurism of the indie scene, searching for something more bold and confident in outlook. As in the previous three decades, the influence of Black America could be heard. The term 'blue-eyed soul' was bandied about and a slew of new bands took to Scottish stages, wooing record company A&R scouts from central London. If the dazzling

Roddy Frame from Aztec Camera, *c.*1985

Pictorial Press Ltd / Alamy Stock Photo

promise of Postcard Records had not been realised, what came next would seriously capitalise on a thriving hotbed of talent. Scotland, particularly Glasgow, seemed to be on fire. Everyone had a quiff, checked shirt, turned-up Levis and a set of clean white socks. Everyone was in a band. As record companies flocked north of the border with cheque books in hand, it was time to shun the underground and make an assault on the mainstream.

Sharing musical DNA and some initial band members, Hipsway and Love and Money brought an injection of unbridled funk to the table that Scotland hadn't seen for a decade. In 1984 Hipsway pulled together ex-members of Altered Images, Johnny McElhone and Grahame 'Skin' Skinner of The Jazzateers into their line-up, with their eyes set on the charts and ears honed to American rhythm'n'blues. Standout single *The Honeythief* set the bar high, scoring a hit on both sides of the Atlantic. But with a moderately successful debut album and a lacklustre follow-up the band split. In 2016 and 2017, however, the fans were rewarded when Hipsway performed to sell-out crowds once again. A new album is also on the cards.

From the remnants of new-wave popsters Friends Again came Love and Money, with guitarist James Grant taking the lead and strutting his stuff up front. With their distinct concept, branding and image in place, Love and Money knocked out brash rockers such as *Candybar Express*, but could also sit back and be more introspective and soulful when required. They were soon snapped up by Phonogram amid an A&R feeding frenzy in Glasgow. With the delayed release of their debut album *All You Need Is Love And Money* and record company indecision, their preliminary buzz and

Love and Money, (left to right) Gordon Wilson, James Grant, Paul McGeechan and Douglas MacIntyre, 1993

Trinity Mirror / Mirrorpix / Alamy Stock Photo

commercial impact dissipated despite a local grassroots fanbase. Smooth production work, slick musicianship and sharp hooks were primed and ready, but the records did not really appeal outwith Scotland. Over a four-album career, Love and Money saw Grant mature into a writer capable of expressing intense melancholy and heart-ache, eventually calling it a day with the band in 1994. Their 1988 work *Strange Kind Of Love* is now seen as timeless in its genre, though Grant these days squirms at his youthful bravado on the band's debut album. Re-forming in 2011, with another album the following year, he now seems far more comfortable in his skin as a mostly acoustic, personal songwriter of depth and quality.

Clydebank quartet Wet Wet Wet were perhaps the embodiment of a new sound and ambition sweeping Scotland in the mid-'80s. They came together at school, playing new-wave covers, taking their name from a Scritti Politti lyric. After two years of rehearsing and writing songs, they emerged sounding as though punk had never happened. Terminally un-hip from the start, the group mined a seam of sweet American soul with a heavy dose of pop, and any rough edges were nicely smoothed away. Singer Mark McLachlan became Marti Pellow and legions of girls

Wet Wet Wet, with Marti Pellow (second left), 1988

Trinity Mirror / Mirrorpix / Alamy Stock Photo

swooned at his charismatic voice and cheeky showbiz smile. Though peers in Glasgow were a bit suspicious of them, Wet Wet Wet would go on to become one of Scotland's most successful and best-loved bands. After an independent start with The Precious Organisation label they signed to Mercury in 1985, but spent two years squabbling about producers, including Memphis legend Willie Mitchell. Debut album *Popped In, Souled Out* finally came out, with a title that riled their competitors, but with chart-bound singles such as *Wishing I Was Lucky*, *Sweet Little Mystery* and *Angel Eyes*. The album itself eventually reached the top spot too – Wet Wet Wet had arrived.

Over a tumultuous career that included Pellow's personal problems with drug and drink dependency, the group notched up a total of three chart-topping albums (out of eight released) and a succession of lucrative tours across the globe. Their singles throughout the '80s, '90s and 2000s were all over the radio too, including the chart-topping Childline charity Beatles cover *With A Little Help From My Friends* in 1988, and the omnipresent *Love Is All Around* in 1994. This Troggs cover famously featured in the box-office smash 'Four Weddings and a Funeral' and saw the group sit at the top of the UK singles chart for a full fifteen weeks until even Pellow, sick of hearing it on the radio, demanded that the single be deleted.

The hits kept coming through thick and thin until around 2008, with the group filling arenas until their finale in 2017. Pellow is now a solo artist and musical actor, while the other band members are still involved in music through session, studio and theatre work. For over three decades pop fans loved the band while the critics baulked, but Wet Wet Wet remain incredibly popular.

Hue and Cry are brothers who also ignored the primitive world of post-punk in favour of soul influences. Pat and Greg Kane from Coatbridge, North Lanarkshire, forged a more cerebral path with a politically-charged, sophisticated pop. Remembered for the acrobatic vocals and pristine hooks of their debut album *Seduced And Abandoned* and top-ten single *Labour Of Love*, their biggest success was the follow-up album *Remote* featuring the more measured *Looking For Linda*. They have made dexterous, jazz-infused pop since 1987 and perform to this day at festivals and on tour. Over the decades Greg has moved further into studio work, whereas Pat has concentrated more on his theoretical and political writing. A supporter of Scottish

Independence and leading light in the 'Yes' movement in 2014, Pat Kane is as well known today as an activist as a musician.

Taking your band name from a Steely Dan song is a way of pinning your musical colours to the mast. Deacon Blue began as a writing vehicle for Dundonian Ricky Ross, blending the heart-on-sleeve, blue-collar songcraft of Bruce Springsteen, the afore-mentioned sophistication of Steely Dan, and Black American soul. With the correct backing musicians and a vocal sparring partner in Lorraine McIntosh – who would eventually become his wife – Ross set his literate musings to an epic musical backdrop. These soon-to-be Scottish psalms somehow managed to keep a foot in the personal and intimate, while also appealing to those who like an emotional sing-along – a secret that many Scottish musicians would master throughout the '80s.

It's no surprise that Deacon Blue became another of the country's most popu-lar acts with their number-one albums and the top-ten single *Real Gone Kid*. With songs like *Dignity*, *Chocolate Girl* and *Fergus Sings The Blues*, the back catalogue is celebrated far and wide. These are songs that resonate with people, and when the

Hue and Cry's Greg and Pat Kane, 1988

group reignited their career in the 2000s, their fans took the journey along with them. All three albums released in the last decade have landed squarely in the top twenty, while Ross has also written songs for the likes of James Blunt, Ronan Keating and Jamie Cullum.

These days Lorraine McIntosh has made a name for herself as an actor, while drummer Dougie Vipond is a now a TV presenter. Ricky Ross continues to write and tour as a solo artist, now focusing on a more acoustic Americana-based sound, and is also busy with the broadcasting of BBC Radio Scotland show 'Another Country'. Like his friend Pat Kane, Ross is a vocal supporter of Scottish Independence in the media and onstage.

Before being signed, local bands Deacon Blue, Wet Wet Wet and Hue and Cry all featured on a compilation cassette, almost an umbrella to an emerging Scottish sound. But more soulful refinement was already evident from a Dundee act that also spawned a renowned songwriter, Gary Clarke. The band Danny Wilson, which had a short run in the latter part of the '80s, had to change its name from Spencer Tracy

Ricky Ross and Lorraine McIntosh of Deacon Blue performing at 'V Festival', Hylands Park, 2013

Wenn Ltd / Alamy Stock Photo

after an objection from the Hollywood actor's estate. At first missing the UK charts but scoring over the Atlantic, *Mary's Prayer* is now a radio and international pop staple. Finally hitting the UK number three, its catchy chorale showed the skills and craftsmanship that would emanate from the band and Clarke in particular. Jazz, soul and syncopated pop were in abundance on the first album *Meet Danny Wilson* (1987), and the follow-up *Bebop Moptop* that hatched another standard in single *The Second Summer Of Love*. The group's career sadly ground to a halt in 1991, but Clarke has gone on to become one of the world's foremost go-to songwriters, crafting pop gems for Natalie Imbruglia, K D Lang and members of the Spice Girls, among others. More recently his work was heard in the film 'Sing Street'. His brother Kit Clarke has embarked on a solo career, while bassist Ged Grimes has moonlighted in Deacon Blue, composed for television, film and video games, and is now a member of Simple Minds.

As the 1980s advanced and dreams and aspirations ballooned, so did the accompanying soundtrack. Often referred to as 'The Big Music', many of Scotland's groups would scale their work to heroic proportions. Composed of minimal song structures, rhapsodic vocal melodies, mournful Celtic touches, huge drum sounds and studio reverb techniques, the new sound was custom-built for large venues.

The Big Music was actually a song featured on the second album *A Pagan Place* by The Waterboys. Mike Scott, previously of Another Pretty Face, formed The Waterboys in Edinburgh in 1983 and has been its only core member until today. The first four albums established him as a literary songwriter with a spirituality uncommon in rock'n'roll. Compared with Van Morrison, Bob Dylan and U2 throughout his career, Scott will be particulary remembered for his anthemic *The Whole Of The Moon*, a passionate tour-de-force. The song drives and emotes with his yearning vocal up front on a huge chorus that invites crowds to chant along. Taken from the third album *This Is The Sea*, it was not a success on first release in 1985 but reaped justifiable rewards on re-release in 1991, winning an Ivor Novello award into the bargain. By the fourth album *Fisherman's Blues*, Scott had veered away from the rock template to include a distinct folk feel, with fiddle riding high in the mix.

Scott has used The Waterboys' name or flown solo across fourteen albums to

create his own bohemian mix of rock and folk. Whether living in Edinburgh, London, New York, Dublin, or the religious retreat of Findhorn in Moray, his influence is obvious in the resurgence of acoustic and traditional music across Scotland and beyond. Bringing it right up-to-date, The Waterboys' *Out Of All This Blue* album went top ten in 2017, demonstrating that Mike Scott is certainly in it for the long haul.

After the relatively messy demise of Fife punks The Skids, the aftermath would see a band eclipse the group's commercial success and quickly build a new army of fans. Guitar maestro Stuart Adamson was keen to stay in his home town of Dunfermline and hooked up with multi-instrumentalist Bruce Watson. Securing a session rhythm section in Tony Butler and Mark Brzezicki, they formed the classic line-up of Big Country, a group that still commands utter devotion. Unashamedly heartfelt and patriotic, lead guitars were soon compared to bagpipes and their melodies imbued with a distinct Celtic flavour. Decked out in plaid shirts, often with saltires

**Mike Scott of The Waterboys, Croke Park,
Dublin, 1986**

Culliganphoto / Alamy Stock Photo

draped across the stage, Big Country's live shows appealed to working-class Scotland and those who wanted the fervour of punk but with a more positive, passionate sensibility. Soon their releases would match that kind of intensity, as the band experienced a meteoric rise. The second single *Fields Of Fire (400 Miles)* went top ten and debut album *The Crossing* did the same in 1983. Perhaps due to indigenous Scots flavours therein, the USA also took to the band, helping another single *In A Big Country* reach the top forty and enabling them to tour there.

Although follow-up album *Steeltown* would top the charts in 1984 and a third album *The Seer* would also guarantee another triumph in 1986, the band were eventually trapped in a musical cage of their own making. Big Country's sound was certainly unique, but it also became a weight they couldn't shake off. Adamson's melodic and lyrical obsessions were somewhat restricting and musicians often have to adapt quickly in the world of pop. Their initial originality would be their undoing

Big Country with Stuart Adamson (second from right), April 1990

Pictorial Press Ltd / Alamy Stock Photo

as fashion slowly drifted away. Fourth album *Peace In Our Time* attempted to break the mould and still went top-ten in 1988, but the band's fortunes were on the wane. Adamson kept the fires burning, maintaining a strong work ethic until the final album in 1999, but tragically took his own life in 2001 as a result of debilitating depression and an ongoing struggle with alcohol. The music world was in shock and long-time fans lost a musical icon. Big Country has since re-formed then, with vocalists The Alarm's Mike Peters, and latterly Simon Hough, keeping Adamson's music and memory alive.

The Silencers were another group that wholeheartedly embraced 'The Big Music', building themselves a stronghold in Scotland and abroad. Taken under the wing of School-house Management, who looked after Simple Minds, they carved out a niche career from 1986–2007. Never quite breaking into the mainstream and fielding comparisons to their Scottish peers and U2, their manifestly traditional influences went down well with European audiences, especially in France.

For stadium rock it was Simple Minds who made the biggest impact globally. Starting the 1980s with post-punk kudos in place, the band's darker underground veneer was soon fused with a more apparent pop dimension and their popularity went stratospheric. The *New Gold Dream (81–82–83–84)* album went to number three and contained bonafide hit singles in *Promised You A Miracle* and *Glittering Prize*. The mid- and late '80s belonged to the band as they conquered the UK, Europe and eventually the USA via a succession of commercial, classy albums, *Sparkle In The Rain*, *Once Upon A Time* and *Street Fighting Years*. Although their pop prowess and

Jim Kerr, with Simple Minds

© Harry Papadopoulos, courtesy Street
Level Photoworks

song-writing skills were now well-tuned, it was actually a Keith Forsey song *Don't You Forget About Me*, used in teen blockbuster film 'The Breakfast Club', which would become their best-known song and key to their breakthrough in the USA.

Simple Minds lived it large. They rivalled U2 at one point, Jim Kerr had a couple of celebrity marriages, and their star shone brightly until the early '90s with *Waterfront*, *Alive And Kicking*, *All The Things She Said* and *Belfast Child* becoming standards. Although their light has never truly dimmed, they did reach a commercial nadir at the start of the 2000s. But with Jim Kerr and Charlie Burchill at their creative core, they have soldiered on and regained considerable ground with their ever-committed fanbase. To date Simple Minds has released an impressive nineteen studio albums, plus various compilations, box sets and live recordings. They even have an album called *Big Music*. Today they must be considered Scotland's most consistently successful and longest-running rock band of all time. Not bad for a bunch of working-class boys from Glasgow.

Straddling the worlds of mainstream, rootsy Scottish pop and the oncoming rush of alternative rock, Del Amitri achieved notable success at home and across the pond. Led by the outspoken, inimitable Justin Currie, this band of school friends came together as a serious proposition in 1983, attracting the attention of new-music guru John Peel and signing to the Chrysalis label. Their debut self-titled collection was jangly, arty and melancholy in sound, but swiftly disappeared from view. After a fan-financed tour in the States and some self-reflection, they began to dabble in overt rock and Americana influences and hit payola on their second album, the top-ten *Waking Hours* from A&M Records. Showcasing Justin Currie's wordplay, song-craft and husky tones, *Nothing Ever Happens* became their signature tune for a while, reaching number eleven in the UK charts before going global. The song was ever-present on radio and television in 1989 and has become a modern busking classic for those pounding the streets armed with an acoustic guitar.

More hits followed including *Kiss This Thing Goodbye*, another smash in *Always The Last To Know* from the equally successful *Change Everything* album, and *Roll To Me* from their fourth long-player *Twisted*. Four of their full-length offerings would reach the UK top ten and the band were one of the few British acts at that time to

make dents in the American top forty on a number of occasions. Their line in smart, country-tinged rock'n'roll certainly struck a chord in the States.

The rest of the '90s was successful for Del Amitri as line-ups fluctuated around the trio of Justin Currie, Iain Harvie and Andy Alston. But after a sixth album in 2002, and almost twenty years in the game, things wound down as Currie invested more time in a solo career and a side-project called The Uncle Devil Show. Like many of their peers, Del Amitri reunited to great acclaim in 2014.

In the 1980s women were still in the minority onstage and upfront, and it was still up to a select few to push the boundaries. One individual who did just that was Bellshill girl Sheena Easton, who went on to become one of Scotland's most successful singers over the decade. While on a scholarship to the Royal Scottish Academy of Music and Drama, she was cajoled into appearing on a 1979 BBC TV show called 'The Big Time'. Though discouraged onscreen by Lulu's manager at that time, Easton would be offered a contract by EMI only a year later and was set to embark

Del Amitri, *c.*1985

Photograph by Jason Tilley
Pictorial Press Ltd / Alamy Stock Photo

on a sky-rocketing career. It began with the top-ten single *Modern Girl*, hotly pursued by a similarly placed hit, *Morning Train (Nine To Five)*. The latter was released in America and topped the charts, giving her instant major success on both sides of the Atlantic. By 1981 Easton had been offered the theme song from the James Bond film 'For Your Eyes Only', which also notched up hits in the UK and USA. Within two years, she had gone from obscurity to global stardom.

As money and opportunity rolled in, Easton relocated to the States and gained dual citizenship. She duetted with Kenny Rogers, worked with esteemed producer and Chic guitarist Nile Rodgers, won a Grammy award, collaborated with Mexican singer Luis Miguel (another Grammy), and in 1987 side-stepped her trademark soft pop for a critically-acclaimed and rather raunchy duet with the megastar Prince. Appearing in his legendary film 'Sign o' the Times' and singing the duet *U Got The Look*, Sheena Easton became the Purple One's muse of the moment. From there she made an album with rhythm'n'blues producers Babyface and Jellybean, and appeared on screen in films and television shows such as the original 'Miami Vice'. With impeccable management she was an unstoppable force in the '80s and to date has sold approximately twenty million records worldwide. More recently, Sheena Easton has taken to the stage in London's West End. Clearly Lulu's manager was quite wrong with his assessment in 1979.

Finnieston-born Sharleen Spiteri has certainly become something of a role-model since exploding onto the international pop scene from 1986 onwards. Her band Texas, featuring ex-Altered Images/Hipsway bassist Johnny McElhone and wunderkind guitarist Ally McErlaine, immediately scored a top-ten hit with the first single *I Don't Want A Lover* in 1989. The debut album *Southside* reached number three in the charts. With their own brand of Americana-drenched, soul-flecked pop, Texas have never looked back. Though experiencing a slight dip in sales and popularity on their second and third albums, the band persevered and toured globally, finally making the album of their careers in *White On Blonde* in 1997. Topping the UK charts, it produced a string of quality singles such as *Say What You Want*, *Halo* and *Black Eyed Boy,* all of which still crop up on radio over twenty years later. To fans old and new, these are modern-day classics.

In a career lasting over three decades to date, Spiteri has proved to be a bold and engaging frontwoman with energy and attitude to spare. She is also regarded as a style icon to many. Despite a few years' hiatus, two Spiteri solo albums and a health scare for McErlaine, the band is undiminished. Spiteri's voice has remained powerful and soulful throughout and Texas has become a veritable hit-machine with three chart-topping albums, thirteen top-ten singles and an astounding forty million albums sold. They are now Scottish pop royalty, keeping their global audience satisfied with regular releases, tours and media coverage.

Eddi Reader, from Anderston, Glasgow, is a free-spirited singer-songwriter who effortlessly flies an empowering flag for women. With a colourful career behind her, she has become a modern-day interpreter of Robert Burns' poetry. Her musical life may have started with busking, but also saw her work for the circus. In the early '80s

Texas, with Sharleen Spiteri, 1989

Photograph by Rudi Reiner
Pictorial Press Ltd / Alamy Stock Photo

she moved to London to sing with post-punks Gang of Four and became a session backing vocalist for a range of artists including Eurythmics and The Waterboys. Her personal public break came via the band Fairground Attraction who went straight to the top of the singles chart in 1989 with the effervescent, shuffling pop of *Perfect*, an aptly-named song. The resulting album *The First Of A Million Kisses* went to number two and the future seemed rosy – until the band split the same year.

Reader was not one to be kept down, however, and went on to appear in the John Byrne television drama 'Your Cheatin' Heart' and get involved in theatre. With the help of Rough Trade label boss Geoff Travis, she embarked on a solo career on the RCA and Warner Brothers labels during the '90s, winning the 'Best Female Singer' Brit award in 1994. Settling with Travis' Rough Trade label in the 2000s, to date she has released eleven albums of largely acoustic folk-pop and accrued a dedicated

Fairground Attraction, with Eddi Reader, 1988

Pictorial Press Ltd / Alamy Stock Photo

fanbase across the UK. Eddi Reader is also well regarded for her renditions of Robert Burns' classics, and her indisputable passion and talent constantly shine through.

Alongside many other like-minded souls, Reader's music pointed towards a back-to-basics attitude, a return to folk traditions – albeit in a modern setting. As the shimmer and shine of the '80s rubbed off on most studio productions, some craved the raw simplicity of an acoustic guitar and an intimate wordsmith. Troubadours such as gravel-throated Dundonian Michael Marra, Motherwell duo The River Detectives and (ex-Bluebells) The McCluskey Brothers all focused on the art of the song and the lyric. This songwriting nous has been central to Scotland's ongoing love affair with music and is hugely significant to subsequent generations. But there is one acoustic duo who certainly overshadow the others – identical twins Craig and Charlie Reid.

Travel the world, ask about Scotland and once 'whisky', 'kilt' and 'Braveheart' are out of the way, the next words could well be 'The Proclaimers'. Ambassadors and gentlemen to the end, Craig and Charlie have enjoyed a musical trajectory that stretches over three decades and ten albums. After playing in local Fife-based punk bands the Leith-born brothers began as an acoustic duo in the '80s and by 1986 had secured a tour support slot with Hull-based indie-popsters The Housemartins – and all on the strength of a basic demo tape. Their raw, emotive, politicised songwriting, close Everly Brothers' blood-harmonies and inherent knack for a catchy tune marked them out immediately. But it was the matching glasses and upfront Scottish accents that really stood out, both at home and abroad. Here was a group that did not shy away from its roots, but actively embraced them. Most acts to this day prefer the Americanised twang of a lead vocal, but not the Reid brothers. Indeed the accent was so pronounced that some thought they might be putting it on for effect. They weren't.

With a Chrysalis Records deal in place, a debut album *This Is The Story* was released in 1987. Tracks such as *Throw The 'R' Away*, *Over And Done With* and the hit single *Letter From America* are all incredible pop nuggets, but also steeped in socio-political reality and romanticism. Their songwriting skills were undeniable and only further confirmed when second album *Sunshine On Leith* was unleashed the following year, including a song that many regard as Scotland's alternative national

Opposite: Craig and Charlie Reid of The Proclaimers, 1987

Trinity Mirror / Mirrorpix / Alamy Stock Photo

anthem – *I'm Gonna Be (500 Miles)*. Possibly no other Scottish song warrants such a huge sing-along in a live context. It has also been used in multiple film and television soundtracks. The title track *Sunshine On Leith* has become a modern standard with real emotional depth. In 2007 songs from *Sunshine On Leith* and other Proclaimers albums were used in a musical of the same name by the Dundee Rep Ensemble. In 2013 a British feature film of the musical was released to plaudits worldwide, giving their songs life way beyond the band itself.

Since the 1980s The Proclaimers have ploughed their own unique musical furrow with superbly crafted songs that encompass rock'n'roll, soul, country, folk and outright pop. Their back catalogue and ongoing songwriting enjoys the praise it deserves, as the duo continue to tour to packed-out halls. Given the subject matter of some of their lyrics, it is perhaps not surprising that the Reid brothers are outspoken supporters of Scottish Independence when asked. After a recent BBC documentary, there is a new album and more touring on the way. It's simple – Craig and Charlie have become national treasures.

There can be no overview of Scottish pop without mention and celebration of Runrig, a band that operates on the edges of 'traditional' music but has that crossover effect. Forming on the Isle of Skye in 1973 around brothers Rory and Calum MacDonald, they have released fourteen studio albums to date and attracted a global following for their fusion of Celtic and rock influences. Widescreen in scale, they would certainly fit into 'The Big Music' category. Lyrically, Runrig has fearlessly

Runrig, Princes Street Gardens, Edinburgh, 1988

championed Scottish history, heritage and the Gaelic language, singing many of their songs in their native tongue.

Neither particularly fashionable nor hip, the band has never compromised and are justified in being considered one of Scotland's best-loved groups. Their most visibly successful period was 1987–97, when signed to the Chrysalis label for five albums. After lead singer Donnie Munro left and was replaced by Nova Scotia song-writer Bruce Guthro, they continued to flourish as an independent, self-contained croft industry. Performing to tens of thousands of fans on world tours and at special 'Beat the Drum' and 'Party on the Moor' shows on home turf, the band has become an institution. They can boast two ex-members who have gone into politics – Donnie Munro for the Labour Party and Pete Wishart (who was also briefly in Big Country) for the Scottish Nationalists. And as they move into their forty-fifth year as an entity, Runrig has finally decided to wrap up an extraordinary career as the world's most successful Gaelic rock group. They will tour throughout 2018 on, most appropriately, 'The Last Dance' – once gone, they will be sadly missed.

Throughout the political turmoil, and against the changing backdrop of 1980s' Britain, Scotland had undoubtedly enjoyed its most glorious, commercial pop moments so far. From pop to funk to stadium rock, some acts achieved more than ever imagined and proved that Scotland could at last compete on a global stage. Whether outwardly nationalist or not, artists were now giving their own culture and identity exposure through music. In reach and in recognition, Scottish pop had finally made its mark. But there was also something bubbling away far underground.

Peoples
march
for jobs

'85

AND ON THE M   H

Chapter six

Upside down

To those at major labels, megastores and promotion companies, the 1980s music business was mainly glitz and glamour, showbiz and shenanigans. Money was beginning to slosh around the economy and life was good for the squeaky-clean, pastel parade of teenagers with mullets, highlights and leg-warmers. Songs of insurrection or rebellion were less likely to be heard on the radio, but rather the sound of smiley, happy, loved-up commerciality. But as with every vinyl record there was a flipside. Running parallel to the omnipresent pop, much of which was hugely entertaining, the decade also became the bedrock for the burgeoning alternative culture – an undercurrent gathering momentum that would see disparate musical underdogs operate below the radar of the mainstream media.

Grabbing hold of the DIY baton, musicians took matters into their own hands, setting up independent labels and collectives. A few would flirt with the charts and conventional stardom, some gaining a few fleeting moments of success, but many shunned them completely. In hindsight the '80s would produce some of the most original and off-kilter sounds Scotland had ever known. This diversity manifested itself in many guises, with unclassifiable mavericks moving into unchartered territory. Musicians were still political but tended not to shout their slogans loud, instead housing anti-establishment principles in art, concepts and lifestyle. For some, consumerism had gone berserk, whereas the late '60s and '70s had promised far more. Musical influences, recording techniques and fashion positioned the rebels against the squares. The streets would soon be filled with punks, goths, indie kids, beatniks, rockers and ravers. The underground was fractured, but it was alive.

This new independent label boom saw shoestring operations spring up in every corner of the UK, enjoying the lifeline of Radio 1 airplay via the champion of weird and wonderful, John Peel. Taking influence from 'The Sound of Young Scotland', Alan McGee was a Glaswegian who did exactly that. As a young musician he had sought solace in punk and played in local bands including The Drains, The Laughing Apple and eventually Biff Bang Pow!. Being a musician though would not define his future.

Pages 98–99: People's March for Jobs,
Scottish Borders, 1983

© The Scotsman Publications Ltd
Licensor www.SCRAN.ac.uk

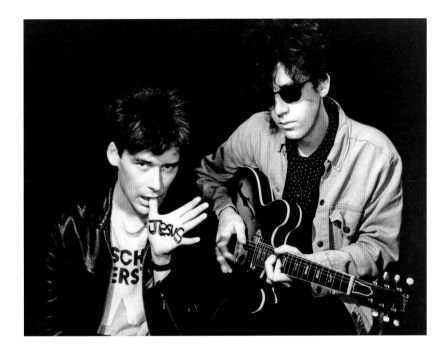

Moving from Glasgow to London in the early '80s to work at British Rail, McGee established The Living Room, an indie club which slowly became a mainstay for waifs and strays who wanted something noisier. At the club's peak in 1983, he decided to start a record label to showcase his favourites who played there. Fledgling to begin with, using self-folded sleeves and cheap seven-inch vinyl, he named it Creation as a homage to the 1960s art-pop band of that name. Creation would go on to enjoy its hey-day and commercial peak for years in the '90s and primarily jumpstarted the careers of three Scottish indie stalwarts – The Pastels, Primal Scream and the label's breakthrough act, The Jesus and Mary Chain.

East Kilbride brothers Jim and William Reid, though a few years apart, grew up in a self-contained bubble of sibling rivalry. They began their career by making home recordings of their songs in 1983, demonstrating a love of punk rock, '60s psychedelia, The Stooges, brutal distortion and the melodic flair of the Beach Boys. When a demo tape was passed to a certain Bobby Gillespie, he recommended

The Jesus and Mary Chain, 1989

Pictorial Press Ltd / Alamy Stock Photo

them to Alan McGee, who immediately booked the brothers for a live show. Though the gig was rumoured to be a chaotic squall-fest and a total disaster, he signed them to Creation. With bassist Douglas Hart and drummer Murray Dalglish, the Reids recorded the feedback-drenched *Upside Down* in 1984. Now regarded as a landmark single, it displayed their resolute vision from the off. It also felt like the first sound since punk that might appeal to disaffected teens. With a nonchalant nihilist streak, the band dressed in black leather and drainpipe jeans with back-combed hair and dark glasses. Like a cross between the Ramones and The Velvet Underground, both musically and visually they were a revelation.

McGee became their manager, Gillespie their drummer, and the band were quickly signed to Warner Brothers. Follow-up singles included *Never Understand*, *Just Like Honey* and *You Trip Me Up*, and in 1985 the inaugural album *Psychocandy* was released to stunned critics and fans alike. Unlike anything before or since, the songs managed to merge caterwauling noise and sugar-sweet melody. Their public image became notorious, with the press proclaiming them the new Sex Pistols. Even their name caused outrage in some circles, and with live performances lasting only fifteen minutes the group showed utter disdain for their audience. There were often mini riots at shows, most famously at North London Polytechnic in March 1985. Despite or maybe because of this, The Jesus and Mary Chain became indie-press darlings.

As they changed stylistically and edged away from the perceived violence and hostile public image, Gillespie left to concentrate on his own band Primal Scream. After heavy touring and internal band pressure throughout 1986, McGee was fired as manager and the brothers entered the studio to make *Darklands* in 1987. Using a drum-machine rather than a live drummer, the results showcased developed songs, more acoustic guitars and further melodic depth. The singles *April Skies*, *Happy When It Rains* and the title track all showed up in the charts. Their early shock value was definitely on the wane and after the tremendous *Sidewalking* stand-alone single the 1989 album *Automatic* was to display a far more electronic feel with hip-hop beats and synthesised bass.

Having peaked in popularity, The Jesus and Mary Chain were an increasingly viable force live, building their set-times to a whopping forty-five minutes. Their career continued as they became mainstays of the expanding alternative scene, eventually disbanding in 1999 after six revered albums of diminishing returns. The duelling brothers did reunite in 2007 for tours and festivals, eventually releasing a seventh album *Damage And Joy* in 2017. Spearheading an indie revolution, The Jesus and Mary Chain is certainly one of the most influential acts to come out of Scotland and copycat bands can still be found around the globe.

Whether bassist in The Wake, drummer in The Jesus and Mary Chain, or singer in Primal Scream, Bobby Gillespie was only ever going to be involved in one thing – rock'n'roll. The Scream, initially the brainchild of Gillespie and Jim Beattie, began their curious journey in Glasgow in 1982, issuing *All Fall Down* as their debut single for Creation. Second single, B-side *Velocity Girl,* was featured on the *New Musical Express C86* compilation tape and their name and reputation grew. Constant line-up changes resulted in Glasgow friends Andrew Innes and Robert 'Throb' Young join-ing, and debut album *Sonic Flower Groove* appeared. Produced at unwarranted expense and mostly derided by critics, it now sounds like a precursor to The Stone Roses' debut with its distinct Byrds influence and chiming guitars.

Tensions within the band eventually split them apart, with Beattie returning to Glasgow to form Spirea X, while Gillespie, Innes and Young moved to Brighton, where they would regroup and recruit session players to work on a second album. This time there was a swing in direction towards '70s Detroit-style heavy rock'n'roll. Too many ballads on this self-titled album made it seem disjointed and again it bombed with the critics. Fans were also confused and the band hunkered down to plan their next move. The Scream then chanced upon a completely revamped style steeped in the advancing sounds of rave culture and their fortunes would be altered forever.

Stephen 'Pastel' McRobbie has been a key figure in independent music in Glasgow for over three decades now. Inspired by proto-primitives such as Swell Maps, Television Personalities and The Modern Lovers, as well as '60s garage bands, his group The Pastels originally came to life as early as 1981. They first teamed up with indie-labels Whaam! and Rough Trade before connecting with Creation for three singles. Throughout many incarnations of the group, Pastel's vision has been that of attitude over technique, with a wilful simplicity and blissful naivety at its centre. With

key member Annabel 'Aggi' Wright at his side, the group released their debut album *Up For A Bit With The Pastels* in 1987 and a second collection in 1989, *Sittin' Pretty*. Katrina Mitchell joined in 1990 and, alongside Stephen, the two still remain at the core of the band today. They made the leap to the nascent Domino Records for their most celebrated works, *Mobile Safari* and *Illumination*, before moving on to compose the soundtrack to David Mackenzie's film 'The Last Great Wilderness' in 2003.

Over their career to date The Pastels have collaborated with many like-minded souls such as Jad Fair and Tenniscoats, and now run the label Geographic, an off-shoot of Domino. After selling records for years in the John Smith's bookshop on Byres Road, Glasgow, during the '80s and '90s, Stephen is now a partner in the excellent Monorail Music record shop. Another cultural landmark for curious music lovers, it is housed in the larger Mono which also serves as a restaurant, bar, gallery and music venue. The Pastels have probably become just as important and valuable as cultural instigators as they are musicians, and Stephen and Katrina have shown themselves to be dedicated, uncompromising supporters of the independent scene in Glasgow

The Pastels

© Harry Papadopoulos, courtesy Street
Level Photoworks

and beyond. They are admired by a select group of music-lovers across the world and their most recent album *Slow Summits* in 2013 was another quiet triumph.

With its roots in independent label culture, a new genre 'indie pop' was born, coming quickly into view in the mid-'80s. *C86*, a cassette tape compiled by the *New Musical Express* paper and bought via mail-order, became a benchmark for this new form of alternative, punky pop, and a loose scene of groups was named after the tape. Anoraks and stripy T-shirts were worn alongside bowl-cuts and hair-clips, with both genders represented in large numbers of the acts on the circuit. Cynics thought it amateur and underachieving, with the words 'twee', 'fey' and 'shambling' bandied about as insults. This only strengthened the fans' love of the sound – and the fashion of course. The musicianship may have been rudimentary and the guitars somewhat jangly, but the songs were good and the genre would prove to be stylistically significant to subsequent eras of independent rock in the UK and USA.

The *C86* tape included many groups from Scotland. Alongside the aforementioned Primal Scream and The Pastels, both of whom shied away from the tag, it also included embryonic recordings by The Soup Dragons, Close Lobsters, the Shop Assistants and The Mackenzies. Unwittingly Scotland was once again at the forefront of a new movement, and labels such as Creation and Stephen Pastel's own 53rd & 3rd were right at the heart of it. The Soup Dragons would go on to have hits and tour the globe in the '90s, but began life as a fizzy pop-punk band in Bellshill, releasing an impressive debut album *This Is Our Art*. Edinburgh's Shop Assistants crafted some wonderful buzzsaw pop gems in their short life, such as the addictive *I Don't Want To Be Friends With You*. And Paisley's Close Lobsters were a slightly more studied affair with two excellent albums, *Foxheads Stalk This Land* and *Headache Rhetoric*, making waves in the UK indie charts and on college radio in the USA.

Industrial petrochemical epicentre Grangemouth may not seem like a hotbed of artistic vision, yet a group making celestial and otherworldly music called it home and would become hugely important in the '80s and '90s. Cocteau Twins were made up of couple Robin Guthrie and Elizabeth Fraser, with original bassist Will Heggie replaced by Simon Raymonde in 1983. Although erroneously allied with the emerging goth scene at the start, they were in fact in a world of their own and delivered a

stunning body of work from 1979–97. Guthrie's shimmering, effects-laden guitar lines would pretty much invent the forthcoming 'shoegaze' sound, Raymonde's bass lines were melodic and rhythmically satisfying, while Fraser sang like no one else before or since. One of the finest vocalists in the history of pop, but perhaps not widely recognised as such, Elizabeth Fraser's imagination, melodic range and phrasing made her unique. As did her decision to forsake singing formed lyrics, preferring sounds and ethereal utterances.

Signing to the inventive 4AD label, Cocteau Twins made eight studio albums and many extended-play records of emotional music that carved out an inimitable niche. You only have to listen to the run of albums – *Blue Bell Knoll* (1988), the chart-bound *Heaven Or Las Vegas* (1990) and *Four Calender Café* (1993) – to experience an exquisite form of new pop unequalled since. Unfortunately the relationship between Fraser and Guthrie disintegrated and by 1997, unable to reconcile their differences, the group self-destructed. Guthrie would have a protracted battle

Cocteau Twins

peteranderson.photos

with alcohol and drugs, eventually getting clean and making music again. Fraser has famously guested with Massive Attack and made solo records, but her appearances are few and far between. Raymonde has become a successful label boss with the superb Bella Union. Original and sorely missed, a rumoured Cocteau Twins reunion was on the cards back in 2005 but alas came to nothing.

The sound of the '80s underground wasn't necessarily scratchy, atonal or avant-garde. The Blue Nile might be seen by some as a more mainstream concern, as they inhabited a musical place polar opposite to indie pop, but they were far more considered, cerebral and soulful than that. Perfectionism isn't quite the word – obsession is more like it. As a studio concern starting in 1981, Paul Buchanan, PJ Moore and Robert Bell signed a single to the label RSO under the tutelage of Calum Malcolm from Castle Sound studio. At the same time, hi-fi producers Linn Products were planning a record label and, after one listen to a track by The Blue Nile, signed the band immediately. With assistance from Virgin Records, Linn Records issued the band's breathtaking debut album in 1984, *A Walk Across The Rooftops*. *Tinseltown In The Rain* was a standout single track and, like the rest of the album, gave the listener a sense of urban alienation, of being an outsider looking in. Heartfelt and haunting with Buchanan's passionate vocal over sparse, synthetic production, the album turned heads across the UK, Europe and the USA.

So began their slow-motion career. The Blue Nile became just as famous for the gaps between their albums, and their distrust of the music industry, as their music. Their refusal to tour, or even appear in public, only served to heighten their mystique and increase the public's desire to see more of them. Eventually a follow-up album *Hats* was released in 1989, five years after their debut. Another impeccable affair, more polished than the last, it won greater acclaim from punters and peers alike, with the single *The Downtown Lights* covered by Annie Lennox. Soon they would play live and tour with friend Ricky Lee Jones, but inevitably disappear from view once again. Buchanan moved to Los Angeles to live and it would be a full seven years before third album, the more acoustic-led *Peace At Last,* was issued in 1996. For their fans the wait between records was excruciating, and after tour dates, a Glastonbury slot and a few television appearances, the band once again vanished into thin air.

Another Blue Nile album did materialise a full eight years later in 2004. Like the previous three, *High* charted and showed that the band's fans were still loyal, in awe of their inimitable talent. But relationships between members of the band were becoming difficult, and an estranged Moore refused to tour and ostensibly left the band. Although there has never been an official announcement, The Blue Nile has never recorded or performed since. Paul Buchanan released an acclaimed solo album *Mid Air* in 2012 and has played live on occasion, but the future is unclear. Look up the definition of 'uncompromising' and 'meticulous' and you'll find The Blue Nile.

Derbyshire-born Lloyd Cole was firmly ensconced at the University of Glasgow, studying Philosophy and Literature, so it was no surprise to hear references made to authors Simone de Beauvoir, Norman Mailer and Truman Capote in his lyrics. Appearing with his group The Commotions throughout Glasgow in 1982, his brylcreemed, beatnik, bohemian aura saw Cole become a favourite of introverted teens and bookish students. Though courted by the label The Precious Organisation, he and the band soon signed to Polydor and released an understated classic in

Blue Nile, with Paul Buchanan (centre), performing at Glastonbury Festival, 1997

Photograph by Martin Norris
Pictorial Press Ltd / Alamy Stock Photo

the 1984 debut *Rattlesnakes*, going top twenty. Combining elements of The Byrds, Velvet Underground, Bob Dylan and contemporaries The Smiths, Lloyd Cole's wistful delivery and ear for a pop-hook saw standout tracks include *Are You Ready To Be Heartbroken?* as well as singles *Forest Fire* and *Perfect Skin*.

The group's next two albums continued their runaway success with *Easy Pieces* (1985) going to number five – including its biggest single *Lost Weekend* – followed by *Mainstream* (1987), likewise reaching the top ten. Lloyd Cole and the Commotions also broke onto the college radio circuit in the USA, shifting decent numbers of records and ensuring Cole's next move would be Stateside. He left The Commotions in 1989 to pursue a solo career in New York City. Since then, as a married father of two, he remains an artist in the music business, with occasional songs placed in Hollywood films. Other Commotions have become session musicians, with bassist Laurence Donegan now a respected journalist and author. Donegan and Cole also share a love of golf, the former as a journalist and the latter as a celebrity player.

In 2016 Cole brought the Commotions' back catalogue to life once again with

Lloyd Cole and the Commotions

Pictorial Press Ltd / Alamy Stock Photo

Glasgow band The Leopards, showing that the songs are still appreciated today. For a while in the '80s though, Lloyd Cole somehow managed to inhabit both the underground and the charts.

Scotland has introduced the world to a number of intriguing eccentrics over its pop history and Nick Currie, a.k.a. Momus, certainly counts as one. Songwriter, journalist, author and conceptualist, originally from Paisley, he has so far released approximately thirty-two albums of off-kilter, intellectualised avant-pop on labels such as Creation and Cherry Red, from debut album *Circus Maximus* in 1986 to the present day. Something of an enigma, with an ardent and dedicated fanbase, his music spans many different genres often using electronica and displaying the influence of iconoclasts such as Jacques Brel and Serge Gainsbourg. Momus has lived in Scotland, London, Paris, Berlin and Tokyo and continues to amuse and confuse in equal measure. He is also the cousin of Justin Currie from Del Amitri.

There were many other unclassifiable bands who floated just below the radar but never quite broke through. After fronting Friends Again, Chris Thomson formed the much-admired chamber-popsters The Bathers. Over their tenure, Thomson and a varying line-up released seven albums via the Go! Discs, Island and Marina labels from 1987–2001. Although many are utterly devoted, a breakthrough remained elusive. Airdrie's The Big Dish was a vehicle for the songs of Stephen Lindsay and his take on slick, pedestrian pop, but they too failed to deliver over their three albums via Virgin and East West records. Kevin McDermott is a singer-songwriter with a Celtic soul and Americana heart who, with his band The Kevin McDermott Orchestra, recorded eight albums over three decades, including their Island Records debut *Mother Nature's Kitchen*. McDermott is still something of a local hero, albeit with modest success.

Bathgate band Goodbye Mr Mackenzie fared better. Changing their name from Teenage Dog Orgy and moving to Edinburgh increased their chances, and a seven-inch single was released on vinyl as part of a Government Youth Training Scheme college course. As they progressed, lead singer and songwriter Martin Metcalfe wrote a bonafide classic in *The Rattler* which scored them an independent chart hit via The Precious Organisation label. Their *Face To Face* EP in 1987 helped to secure a major label deal with Capitol Records and it looked like the band's future was set. With

Metcalfe upfront, Shirley Manson on keyboards and vocals, and former The Exploited guitar-slinger 'Big' John Duncan in their ranks, they blended the feral nature of punk, arty intelligence and effortless pop melodies. Three albums were released and the band toured far and wide. A re-released *The Rattler* went top forty and debut album *Good Deeds And Dirty Rages* top thirty in 1989, but the stars did not properly align for the band. By 1992 they had morphed into another group, Angelfish, with Manson as singer. The Mackenzies would try to regain ground, but by 1996 any semblance was extinguished. Metcalfe would go on to form The Filthy Tongues in due course, while Manson joined American rockers Garbage and has since become a global star.

Overground pop and underground indie may have dominated the '80s, but other genres were also at play. Hard rock or prog never dies, and with the 'New Wave of British Heavy Metal' appealing to large swathes of youth there was a new hunger for it. The critics may have wanted to rewrite history and pretend it didn't exist, but the music-buying public wasn't letting go. British rock band and Tolkien-inspired Marillion were continually pilloried by the press, but enjoyed great success thanks largely to their first frontman and co-songwriter Derek William Dick – known as Fish.

Marillion, *c.*1988

Photograph by Rudi Reiner
Pictorial Press Ltd / Alamy Stock Photo

Influenced by Genesis, Yes and The Sensational Alex Harvey Band, the Dalkeith-born singer joined the Aylesbury band in 1981 and this would prove to be the group's most successful time in terms of chart placements and radio play. Across four top-ten albums – *Script For A Jester's Tear*, *Fugazi*, number-one *Misplaced Childhood* and *Clutching At Straws* – the band became highly popular with hits such as *Kayleigh* and *Lavender*, as well as reviving the fortunes and image of prog rock. Marillion built up a legion of followers and were an inspiration to future generations, but at the peak of their powers Fish left the band to pursue a solo career under his aquatic pseudonym. He has now branched out into acting and radio-presenting.

GUN were rockers with a definite Glasgow edge. Formed in 1987 they signed to A&M records a year later. With four top-forty albums and tours supporting The Rolling Stones, Def Leppard and Bon Jovi, they enjoyed a ten-year blast, demonstrating that not only were Scots capable of turning the guitars up but could create hits as well. Titles such as *Taking On The World*, *Gallus* and *Swagger* oozed confidence for their radio-friendly rock. Their biggest hit was a cover of Cameo's *Word Up!* which upped the ante and went top ten, but a selection of their own numbers such as *Better Days* and *Don't Say It's Over* also charted, adding to the group's longevity. With their line-up fluctuating and a decline in fortunes after an over-produced fourth album, GUN split in 1997. Coming back together in a different configuration in 2008, they have made another four albums and kept the flag flying to an enthusiastic response.

Punks Not Dead was the studio debut of The Exploited in 1981. Though the initial impact of punk had subsided and fashion moved on, its ferocity and anti-

GUN, *c.*1990

Pictorial Press Ltd / Alamy Stock Photo

authoritarianism still permeated youth culture. It hadn't died but gone hard-core, splintering into micro-genres. Many different versions appeared, keeping it fresh. Truly underground proponents of a new form were Stretchheads, a band from Erskine who even now sound extreme. They took the speed and anger of punk, but intertwined spasmodic jazz elements and surreal, abrasive humour, while wearing gas-masks, balaclavas and Hawaiian shirts onstage. Two albums, including the interestingly titled *Five Fingers, Four Thingers, A Thumb, A Facelift And A New Identity* confirmed them as a pioneering if antagonistic noise combo from 1987–91.

The Dog Faced Hermans were partners in this off-kilter musical anarchism. Like the Stretchheads they won the praise of John Peel who booked both bands to play studio sessions. The Hermans were from Edinburgh and made genuinely odd but entrancing music that blended punk, jazz, folk and noise over six albums. Always on tour and active in their mission to subvert hearts and minds, they played across Europe, America and Canada, finally relocating to Amsterdam to be near musical soulmates The Ex. In their decade together, the Hermans showed the potential of improvised, politicised music with a real sense of freedom.

Traditional music is in Scotland's blood of course, and always close by in pubs, clubs or radio. In the '80s some musicians took the incentive from punk to create a thrashy, wild, untamed type of folk. Ayrshire brothers Stephen and David Wiseman became the Nyah Fearties and released six albums, helped along by Irish-British The Pogues. We Three Kings from Edinburgh put out a handful of independent releases and were championed by The Waterboys. And Swamptrash crashed bluegrass into rockabilly/punk combo psychobilly and won a fervent following, before morphing into the globetrotting Celtic fusion kings Shooglenifty.

Many lambast the 1980s as a period of superficiality, indulgence and watered-down art, but in fact the doors had been blown off and anything was possible. The next genuine innovation, however, was music made using computers. Nothing had been socially or culturally revolutionary since punk – until the arrival of acid house and the accompanying rave culture that began to show its smiley face across the UK in the latter part of the decade. Originating in the black and gay club scenes of Chicago, this mutant offshoot of disco felt fresh and new with its 4/4 kick-drum beats, minimalist electronic bass lines and piano stabs. By the late '80s, house music was taking over and Scotland was quick to get on board. Clubs sprang up all over and slowly DJs, producers and bands incorporated the genre into their own sets.

Aberdeen band The Shamen were formed in 1986 with an obsessive love of '60s psychedelia. Their debut album *Drop* was a trippy, acid-drenched rock album, but showed the band's lysergic intentions. Soon frontman and main songwriter Colin Angus was joined by partner in crime Will Sinnott, both becoming entrenched in the emerging rave scene and introducing electronic production, synthesisers and sampling techniques to the group. The album *In Gorbachev We Trust* and mini-album *Phorward* followed, showing a transition from indie combo to an increasingly house-tinged outfit. Moving to London, they toured with budding DJs and other electronic acts as part of the groundbreaking 'Synergy' package, and when their *En-Tact* album was released in 1990 on the One Little Indian label it featured additional production and remixes from the likes of Paul Oakenfold, Steve Osbourne and Graham Massey. Their evolution into an almost entirely electronic act was complete and the album saw them hit the top forty for the first time. Single *Pro>Gen* would be re-released as *Move Any Mountain* and make it to number four. The Shamen had arrived, but tragedy stuck when Sinnott drowned while swimming off the coast of Spain.

In deciding to continue Angus discovered that their initial breakthrough was leading towards chart domination. The Shamen embraced pop with their friend Mr C joining full-time and taking lead vocals on key tracks for the next album *Boss Drum* in 1992. Their biggest hit, which stayed at the top for four weeks, was controversial, with *Ebeneezer Goode* containing a barely disguised reference to the Class A drug Ecstasy. With a video featuring Glaswegian shock-comedian Jerry Sadowitz and its addictive chorus, the song remains their best-known track.

As with many who have enormous chart success and drift from their underground roots, The Shamen found it difficult to follow *Boss Drum*. Receding from view over another three albums and experimentation with the then embryonic internet, Angus ended the group in 1999. But as an example of rave culture going overground and breaking into people's consciousness, The Shamen showed it could happen.

A more dissident affair, Edinburgh-based Finitribe began in 1984 as a guitar band releasing an EP and securing a John Peel session, before giving up their rockist roots for the new technology of samplers and electronics to reinvent their sound. The single *De-Testimony*, with its clanging bell samples and distinctive hook, was a cult classic and infiltrated the flourishing house scene. After releases on the industrial label Wax Trax in Chicago, original member Chris Connelly left to join US bands Ministry and Revolting Cocks. Davie Miller, John Vick and Philip Pinsky continued, as Finitribe moved in more dance-orientated directions and set up label Finiflex to release album *Noise, Lust And Fun*. Soon signed to the One Little Indian label, the more conceptual *Grossing 10k* album was released. As a production team they were absorbed into the club scene, enjoying success with their excel-

lent album *An Unexpected Groovy Treat* (1992), with blissed-out Balearic singles such as *Forever-green* and *101* produced by the dub-house supremo Andrew Weatherall.

Finitribe then flitted between labels and management with band members coming and going, finally winding up the project by 2000. More importantly though, they set up their Finiflex label and studio in Leith, Edinburgh, giving them control over their musical destiny. The studio is now run by John Vick and makes high-end sound design and music for television, film and computer games. Over the years, the label has released music from Scottish acid-house pioneer Ege Bam Yasi, Justin Robertson, and even the American pop/rock band Sparks. But with the core of Miller and Vick back in action, now known as Finiflex, there is a new album in the pipeline.

Across fragmented genres many acts gained notoriety and moderate success, but their alternative ideas paved the way for what was next. In the '90s, the underground was set to go mainstream.

Finitribe, with Davie Miller (left) and Philip Pinski (right), 1992

Martyn Goodacre / Getty Images

Chapter seven

in a big country

The very essence of a country's music community is its live audiences and gig-going public. Scotland is constantly referred to as having the best crowds in the world by touring acts and its homegrown artists. You can criss-cross the globe only to find that a swaying, singing Glasgow crowd beats the lot. Like nowhere else on earth, Scotland enjoys a party and is proud of that fact. It is certainly true that there has been a wide range of live venues across the country through the decades, and therein fans have come alive to each generation's individual soundtrack. From folk clubs to stadia, concert halls to pubs, the ticket stubs, crowd photos and neon signs are testament to how we experience music in its rawest, most direct and exciting form within some truly infamous nightspots.

Around forty active dance halls and ballrooms kept their doors open after the Second World War, creating a network throughout the land. Edinburgh had the Palais, Assembly Rooms and New Cavendish, among others. Glasgow folk went to the Barrowland Ballroom, Dennistoun Palais, Green's Playhouse and the Locarno. Dance-goers in Aberdeen headed for the Beach Ballroom. Dundee had the impressive Caird Hall and Empress Ballroom, Alloa had its Town Hall, Inverness the Northern Meeting Rooms, Elgin the Assembly Rooms, while the Perth City Hall, Hamilton Trocadero and Ayr Pavilion kept the locals on their toes. The legacy of these buildings continues to this day in Scotland, with some still around to galvanise those wishing to shake off their weekly woes amid a crowd of friends.

As the 'big band' sound streamlined and gave way to its wilder, noisier offspring rock'n'roll, towns and cities had to accommodate the avalanche of new acts. With smaller groups and more simplistic, stripped-back music, it was far easier to perform in a village hall, coffee shop or community centre. Soon specific nightclubs would pop up to accommodate the growing crowds. Throughout the 1960s and into the '70s, Edinburgh alone had The Kasbah, Bungy's, The Tempo Club, The Gamp, The Place, McGoo's and The Combination. These provided spaces for rhythm'n'blues, beat and soul fans to meet, drink and cut loose to the new sounds of The Who, The Spencer

Pages 116–17: The Waterboys at The
Electric Picnic Music and Arts Festival,
Stradbally, County Laois, Republic of
Ireland

Barry Cronin / Alamy Stock Photo

Davis Group, The Troggs, and many more. Folk revivalists would also have their strongholds at Glasgow's Scotia bar and Clive's Incredible Folk Club out west, and Edinburgh's Howff Club and Crown Bar in the east.

Scotland may have been a step or two behind London in these embryonic times, but even north of the Border music and fashions moved quickly. Some clubs swiftly seemed old hat and were demolished or rebranded for the next wave of teenagers and twenty-somethings looking for loud music and cheap thrills. As pop became a viable commodity – shifting thousands of records and proving its undoubted long-evity as an artform – the acts needed larger places to play. The main cities drew the touring talent, so musicians and fans gravitated towards them, with The Beatles, The Rolling Stones, The Animals and their ilk dropping into Edinburgh's Usher Hall or the Odeon Cinema in Glasgow. By the dawn of the 1970s these venues, and others such as the Leith Citadel Theatre, would soon house the progressive and heavy rock acts that followed, including Led Zeppelin, Pink Floyd and Deep Purple.

When discussing legendary Scottish venues, however, it is The Apollo in Renfield

Archie Fisher at The Howff Club,
Advocate's Close, Edinburgh, 1962

© National Museums Scotland

Street, Glasgow, that still inspires awe, reverence and sheer delight. Previously known as Green's Playhouse, which hosted incredible performances by Jimi Hendrix and Miles Davis, it would change ownership, enjoy some minor refurbishment and become a touring rock mecca, re-opening as The Apollo in 1973. Known locally as the 'Purple Palace', The Rolling Stones played two fabled nights there; and local heroes The Sensational Alex Harvey Band packed the place on many occasions, including a string of three sell-outs in December 1975. Status Quo, Thin Lizzy, The Clash, Blondie, and countless others, performed memorable shows there; but when AC/DC released their stunning 1978 live album *If You Want Blood, You've Got It*, recorded in The Apollo, the sound of the 'Glasgow choir', as the local audience was known, could be heard in all its glory. With tales of rowdy and impassioned crowds, and how the balcony would visibly move up and down as they bounced, the venue is steeped in myth and merriment. In many ways The Apollo gave modern Glasgow its musical soul, but after twelve monumental years it eventually crumbled and was left to rot, sadly closing its doors in 1985. Two years later its was gutted by a rogue fire.

Opposite and above: The Beatles at Caird Hall, Dundee, 1964

© National Museums Scotland

At the end of the '70s with the arrival of punk, a new set of grassroots venues appeared. The music was back-to-basics and groups were still trying to find their feet. Like its emerging DIY label scene, Scotland truly began to blossom at this time. Initially Glasgow held on to its dirty-denim, hard rock reputation for a while. But with the Lord Provost banning punk from the city, if you couldn't get over to Edinburgh for your new-wave kicks then the main supporters of the scene were to be found in nearby Paisley. The Silver Thread Hotel and Bungalow Bar are now recognised for their illustrious punk credentials with Generation X, Buzzcocks, The Rezillos, and other acts, passing through their hallowed doors.

Edinburgh saw the cream of the crop play its mid-sized venues, revelling in its reputation as an international tour destination. Previously known as the Pentland Club in the '60s, Tiffany's in Stockbridge became a hive of punk, reggae and new-wave activity with Iggy Pop, Elvis Costello, Steel Pulse and the Two Tone Tour playing its stage. The White Elephant Club, which had booked acts such as Slade and Writing on the Wall, changed its name to Valentino's to play host to bands like Adam & the Ants, The Cure and The Fall. Spoilt for choice, Edinburgh also had Clouds (later known as Coasters and then The Network) and The Nite Club on Greenside Place next to The Playhouse, welcoming to Scotland U2, Depeche Mode, Ramones, The Damned, Dexy's Midnight Runners, and many more. Perhaps the most influential of all punk gigs in Scotland took place in the Edinburgh Playhouse itself. The Clash's 'White Riot' package tour in 1977 saw The Jam, The Buzzcocks, Subway Sect, The Slits, as well as the headliners, instigate a Scottish post-punk revolution in

Glasgow Apollo after the fire, 1988

its grand surroundings. Members of Orange Juice, Josef K, and the Fire Engines were all in attendance and experienced an epiphany.

Taking the place of The Apollo in the hearts of Glasgow audiences is the Barrowland Ballroom ('Barrowlands' or simply the 'Barras'). A venue with three separate lifetimes, it was originally built above its famous market in Glasgow's east end in 1934 to house the dance bands of the era. In 1958 the venue shockingly burned to the ground, but reopened again in 1960 to nurture the rock'n'roll generation and beat boom with a sprung dance-floor and star-encrusted, curved ceiling. Falling into disrepair due to stiff competition, it was mothballed by the late '70s, though very briefly revived as a roller-disco in 1981. When Edinburgh promoters Regular Music were on the hunt for somewhere to stage a concert and video-shoot for the Simple Minds' breakthrough hit *Waterfront* in 1982, the dusty, vacant Barrowlands and its spectacular neon sign were ignited once more.

The Barrowlands has continued at pace to this day, with innumerable gigs and very little refurbishment. Its atmosphere and vibe have gained a worldwide reputation with artists as diverse as Foo Fighters, Steve Earle and Public Enemy all singing its hallelujahs. Various songs have been written about it, and the Ulster rockers Stiff Little Fingers have played there on St Patrick's Day every year since 1992. All Scottish bands of any standing would rather play the Barras than anywhere else on earth, and recently Frightened Rabbit, The Twilight Sad, Young Fathers and streetwise song-writer Gerry Cinnamon have had that honour. It is a veritable Glasgow institution and if ever threatened with closure there would be riots on the streets.

Neon sign of the Glasgow Barrowland Ballroom

Seizing the day and wrestling the hipster crown from Edinburgh, Glasgow's pop renaissance came in the post-punk '80s, thanks to the influence of Postcard Records and the consequent overground explosion of talent throughout the city. Its Strathclyde and Queen Margaret University unions would become hotbeds for rock'n'roll insurrection; whereas Night Moves on Sauchiehall Street would soon showcase touring indie, punk and goth *alumni*, seeing The Smiths, Cocteau Twins, Aztec Camera and Marillion all pass through. The hugely influential club Splash One at 46 West George Street was co-run by Primal Scream's Bobby Gillespie. The venue held the first Scottish shows for Sonic Youth and Wire, as well as local heroes The Pastels and BMX Bandits throughout 1985/86. These nights would grow in legend and stature over the coming years, encouraging others to carry its psychedelic punk mantle onwards.

As the 1990s rolled on, there was no stopping Glasgow as a proliferation of trailblazing venues burst through its city centre. The 13th Note on Glassford Street took the politicised DIY nature of anarcho-punk and vegetarianism to its bosom, becoming a counter-culture outpost for future members of Bis, The Delgados, Mogwai and Franz Ferdinand. Nice'n'Sleazy was a breeding ground for Arab Strap, Snow Patrol and Astrid to play shows and drink pints. The Cathouse and The Garage would be surrogate homes to the black-clad rock hoards, as the Sub Club and Arches became Glasgow's club-culture nucleus.

One venue gained all the headlines though, due to the names that would grace its stage and its alignment with Scotland's biggest promoters DF Concerts. King Tut's Wah Wah Hut cheekily pinched its name from a New York nightclub and opened its doors on St Vincent Street in 1990. It would become infamous as the place Alan McGee signed Oasis, arguably the biggest UK band of their generation, but Beck, Blur, Charlatans, Travis, Manic Street Preachers, Radiohead, Muse, The Killers and many more would also perform there. The club's policy of treating touring acts well stood them in good stead, with beer and a square meal provided to artists as part of the deal (rare at the time for a grassroots venue). When the name King Tut's was emblazoned on the side of a stage at the country's biggest pop festival, its kudos rose even higher.

Since then Glasgow's live music status has only increased. Today it is a music tourist destination, due to some of the aforementioned venues and a slew of new ones such as Bloc and Broadcast; the vegan-friendly 13th Note offshoots, Mono and Stereo; massive halls such as the SECC, and more recently The Hydro; and the newly-opened art and club warehouse, SWG3. As the UK's third most happening music city after London and Manchester, Glasgow is booming like never before.

Edinburgh, however, has lost a little of its mojo when it comes to contemporary music. In the '90s and 2000s, The Venue and Calton Studios (later Studio 24) were on the nationwide circuit and booked innumerable international names including Nirvana, Smashing Pumpkins, Fugazi and The Strokes, while housing such renowned club nights as 'Pure' and 'Sativa'. The Playhouse, Picture House, Café Graffiti, The Bongo Club and La Belle Angele all catered for rock, pop, funk, soul and hip hop to indigenous music-lovers and the city's transient student population. Some of these venues are sadly no more – and while still healthy, Edinburgh's scene today is not what it was. With property and development space at a premium, the artists have fewer places to go. Music does flourish, however, in bijou venues like the Leith Depot, Sneaky Pete's, Bannerman's and Henry's Cellar Bar, as well as medium-sized venues such as The Liquid Room and Queen's Hall. Of course the capital has the annual Edinburgh International Festival and Fringe, but sometimes people forget it's a year-round music city.

Looking beyond the central belt, Inverness books an array of music across assorted locations like The Market Bar, Ironworks and Eden Court Theatre; Stirling keeps its cutting edge at the Tolbooth; Dundee has Beat Generator, the Reading Rooms, and the Caird Hall as the jewel in its crown; while Aberdeen boasts a great selection with The Lemon Tree, Café Drummonds, the Tunnels and the revamped Beach Ballroom.

Although outdoor rock festivals came into existence in the '60s and would continue throughout the next decade in a bid to recreate the magic of the Wood-stock Festival and the Isle of Wight, they were still very much fledging affairs in terms of structural organisation, hygiene, safety and tickets sales. 'Free' festivals were applauded and encouraged, but future generations would actually sneer at such events as a viable way to perform in public, due to inadequate PA equipment and staging problems. The '80s saw this slowly change as Knebworth, Donnington and Reading catered for fields of heavy-metal fans. But as the hip, indie and post-punk listeners warmed to the promise of alternative festivals, such events would proliferate in the '90s and way beyond. Aside from random events like The Grangemouth Festival in 1972 and Loch Lomond Rock Festival in 1979, there was little appetite from promoters. Perhaps they thought Scotland was simply too dreich to enjoy music alfresco.

As the 1980s took hold and 'The Big Music' became its soundtrack, venues needed to adjust to the legions of fans themselves. Organisers started to look at sports arenas as a genuine alternative. Here you could create the atmosphere of a national football or rugby game, and make an extremely lucrative one-off spectacle for the groups in question. Over the years Edinburgh's Murrayfield Stadium has hosted U2, David Bowie and The Rolling Stones; Hampden Football Ground in Glasgow has enjoyed Paul McCartney and AC/DC; and Ranger's Ibrox Stadium once presented Simple Minds to a crowd of dedicated Celtic fans. As the quality of sound-systems improved, security tightened and the necessary toilet and food areas were developed, realisation dawned that outdoor Scottish gigs could actually work.

In 1994 DF Concerts affiliated themselves to the Tennents brewing company and 'T in the Park' became the country's first annual national pop gathering, booking Rage Against the Machine and Primal Scream as its headliners. Quickly rivalling the existing WOMAD and Reading festivals in the south of England, it would soon be second only to Glastonbury in size at approximately 85,000 people. As in The Apollo Theatre or Barrowlands, crowd reaction was loud and enthusiastic. They jumped as one and sang as one. Every act wanted to take in 'T in the Park' as part of a tour, and for local musicians it became a rite of passage to play or attend. Nowadays, as 'festival season' and its many competitors are taken for granted, Scotland's summer has multiple outdoor events happening every weekend. But by producing a world-class event and keeping both mainstream and alternative music-lovers close to home, 'T in the Park' was a true pioneer. In many ways, it put Scotland on the map.

Over the past two decades, inner city festivals have sprung up to great acclaim, including Triptych, Stag & Dagger and the increasingly important Celtic Connections.

Out in the flat field the likes of Wickerman, Belladrum, Connect, Loopallu, Rock-Ness and Electric Fields have entertained the masses. More recently the trend has seen gatherings on city green spaces – hence Gig on the Green, Indian Summer, Bellahouston Park, Kelvingrove Bandstand and 'T in the Park's' Glasgow successor, TRNSMT. And don't forget one of the biggest street parties on earth – Edinburgh's Hogmanay.

Whether indoor or out – pub, club or arena – the Scots certainly have an inbuilt desire to commune, sing, dance and be part of a like-minded tribe; to experience that camaraderie and trust; to be able to laugh, cry, hug, let go and enjoy themselves – no matter the consequences. Live music creates the perfect environment to do exactly that and Scotland is masterful at it.

RockNess festival, Inverness-shire

Ross Gilmore / Alamy Stock Photo

Chapter eight

Bandwagonesque

As the 1990s rolled in, the consequences of unregulated capitalism may have started to reap rewards for business, but mid-way through the decade Britain was in the mood for change. Pop music was a bigger industry in the country than ever before and accounted for vast exports. It could not be ignored and was a continuing influence on social and political issues. Concerned about the mushrooming rave culture, the Government tried to implement a Criminal Justice and Public Order Act 1994 which prompted a nationwide campaign against it. Groups of young people were to be dissuaded from dancing and communing in open fields, regarded as a risk to the country's law and order.

'Legal' festivals began to proliferate across the United Kingdom, and it was no different in Scotland. In 1994 'T in the Park' became the first annual event to rival the existing Glastonbury and Reading rock festivals held in the south of England. 'Festival season' and its competitors are now taken for granted, but as a way of keeping mainstream and alternative music punters close to home, 'T in the Park' was a true pioneer.

By 1997 a 'New Labour' victory and the self-assurance brought about by 'Britpop' stoked optimistic fires. By the end of the decade there would be Devolution for Scotland and the country's own Parliament. What's more, Scottish artists were now resisting London's magnetic pull and deciding to stay put to develop their careers. Somehow the impossible was beginning to seem possible.

Many of the big players from the previous decades had begun to take a back seat. They had made their mark and certainly put Scottish pop on the map. As they were maturing, starting families and winding down that essential drive and ambition, it was the optimum time for underdogs to raise their heads above the parapet and push music in a different direction. If the foundations had been laid post-punk, the next few years would see the culmination of years of underground toil as many subcultures entered the public consciousness. Alternative music in its various forms would go global, with dance and indie rock muscle entering the charts, fashion and politics.

Pages 128–29: Coloured powder is thrown at the Belladrum Tartan Heart Festival, 2014

Sam Kovak / Alamy Stock Photo

If escapism had largely been the order of the day in the 1980s, then a new sense of realism, grit and purpose was next.

As a direct reaction to bombastic Los Angeles 'poodle-rock' and clean-cut, chart-dominating pop, a visceral new American form of rock called 'grunge' began to take hold. The new movement seemed to stem mainly from the rainy west-coast city of Seattle and brought with it a return to untamed guitars and intense, raw vocals. Alternative genres such as punk, heavy metal and '60s psychedelia were the touch-stones for this new generation who declared their no-nonsense approach to song-writing and showmanship. Gone was the glitter and polish in favour of plaid shirts and ripped jeans. Hair grew long again, as the nihilism of punk was coupled with the dirty denim of '70s rock. Names such as Green River, The Melvins, Mudhoney, Tad, Screaming Trees and Nirvana appeared in the music press as the metaphorical match lit the touchpaper.

Into grunge's mix of influences was the 'C86' movement and Scotland's alter-native bands in particular. Mudhoney were vocal in their appreciation of The Green Telescope and The Thanes, splendid beat combos from Edinburgh who revived the glorious garage sounds of the mid-'60s; while scene trailblazers Nirvana professed their undying love for a Glasgow duo called The Vaselines. During their brief time together from 1986–90, The Vaselines would release two EPs and an album *Dum Dum* on the 53rd & 3rd label, but to little fanfare. A select indie-pop crowd enjoyed them, but sales were frugal. Songwriters Eugene Kelly and Frances McKee would see their personal fortunes completely change, however, when three of their uncompli-cated anthems were affectionately covered by a certain uber-fan, Kurt Cobain.

Armed with a voice that could strip wallpaper and the most brutal of guitar sounds, Cobain was enamoured by the simplicity and directness of The Vaselines' songs. He constantly espoused his love of 'shambling' indie pop and the anti-machismo of the scene, saying how it shaped his own songs. As the band crossed over to large audiences, he repaid the favour by taking Kelly's new band Eugenius on tour with Nirvana, bringing him onstage to sing Vaselines' songs at key live shows. Since then Kelly has had the resources and time to pursue a solo career and has always recognised his debt to Cobain. In 2006 The Vaselines re-formed for a one-off

show and subsequently decided to make it into a more serious affair once again. They issued their complete discography for the Sub Pop label, originally the backbone of the grunge movement, and released two albums in 2010 and 2014 to a world-wide fanbase.

Nirvana had other Scottish connections, employing road-crew from Scotland, in particular Edinburgh, a city they fell in love with. The Exploited and Goodbye Mr Mackenzie guitarist 'Big' John Duncan became the group's guitar technician and occasionally joined the band onstage as second guitarist. This crew would accompany Nirvana on their explosive rise to the top as they reinvented rock for a new era. In 1994 it would all come to a terrible and premature end when Kurt Cobain took his own life. Many of the Nirvana crew remain in the music business alongside enduring acts such as The Melvins and Foo Fighters, whose long-standing monitor engineer Ian Beveridge is still in the fold.

Along with acolytes Dick Green and Joe Foster, Creation's Alan McGee was watching from London and was quick to snap up some of Scotland's new noise-

Eugene Kelly with Kurt Cobain of Nirvana,
Reading Festival, 23 August 1991

Mick Hutson / Getty Images

mongers for the label. It became apparent that many of the groups had a similar genesis and emanated from the area of Bellshill, a suburb of Glasgow near Mother-well. These groups managed to distil the 'C86' jangle, the essence of '60s melody-smiths The Byrds and the heft of grunge to create a song-based counterpart to the 'shoegaze' movement down south.

Central to the Bellshill scene was a band associated with 'C86' without having actually been on the *NME* compilation. BMX Bandits formed in 1985 and shared DNA with The Vaselines, The Boy Hairdressers, Superstar and The Soup Dragons, as members of these bands started their musical lives alongside BMX frontman and songwriter Duglas T. Stewart. Stewart was a true eccentric, ready to unleash his raw, romantic and often humorous view of the world on an unsuspecting public. It could be said that BMX Bandits became the archetypal indie pop band and have been celebrated across the world ever since. After a few early releases on the 53rd & 3rd and Vinyl Japan labels, the group was signed to Creation, helping them to achieve their most noticeable successes – singles *Serious Drugs* and *Kylie's Got A Crush On Us*

Eugene Kelly of The Vaselines performing at Liverpool Static Gallery, 18 September 2010

WENN Ltd / Alamy Stock Photo

from 1992/93. With three albums for the label throughout the '90s, and many more via other labels since, the band became cult-heroes and have never relinquished that mantle. Stewart has kept BMX Bandits going with a roll-call of musicians, making it a veritable who's who of the Bellshill indie mafia. Their most recent album in 2017, *Forever*, says it all.

As grunge took hold, Scotland's indie scene turned up the distortion on their guitars. Labels such as 'twee' could no longer be applied to bands who could assault your eardrums in such an uncouth manner. The leading light from Bellshill would be a band who that go on to transcend genre-classification and evolve into one of Scotland's favourite ever groups, Teenage Fanclub. Described by the aforementioned Cobain as the 'greatest band in the world', they formed in 1989 and were quickly taken under the wing of the emerging alt-rock scene in the States. Their original, chaotic sound occupied the same sonic space as the American grungers, especially on their debut album *A Catholic Education* (1990) and subsequent *The King* (1991). It was a shot in the arm to the Scottish scene and saw a parade of copycats strap on guitars around Glasgow. But the 'Fannies' proved to be more nuanced and subtle than many of their peers in the long run. With three singer-songwriters – Norman Blake, Gerard Love and Raymond McGinley – each performing lead vocals on their own tunes, the quality control was always high. A succession of drummers – Francis MacDonald, Brendan O'Hare and Paul Quinn – also added class to the musical mix.

Their third album *Bandwagonesque* cemented their reputation as national treasures. Clinching the top album spot ahead of Nirvana's *Nevermind* in the influential *SPIN* magazine 1991 end-of-year poll, it showcased the marriage of noisy guitars and jubilant melodies on tracks such as *What You Do To Me*, *Star Sign* and *The Concept*, with musical nods to Neil Young and Big Star. The album went to number twenty-two in the charts and Scotland had a new rock band to sit alongside its US counterparts. The Fanclub's trajectory accelerated as the album *Thirteen* ironically went to number fourteen in 1993; and their masterpiece album *Grand Prix* hit number seven in 1995. Another superb album *Songs From Northern Britain* followed in 1997, itself a cheeky aside to Britpop, which got as far as number three, their

highest chart position to date. Alan McGee's Creation label had now released five acclaimed albums and had one of the best-loved bands in the country on its books. Teenage Fanclub were on peak form and had found their niche, with a well-defined Americana influence creeping into their sound. Their increasingly acoustic and lyrically romantic songs were rightly held in high regard by the next wave of bands watching from the wings.

Indie rock had now fully infiltrated the charts, hearts and minds of the nation's youth, and the humble, self-effacing Fanclub were unsuspecting torchbearers. Contrary to their DIY attitude and indie philosophy, however, the Fanclub did live briefly on a major label when Sony bought out Creation following the enormous success of indie behemoths Oasis. The resulting album *Howdy* in 2000 would be, bizarrely, their lowest chart placement for a decade at number thirty-three, but was

Teenage Fanclub, *c.*1990

Pictorial Press Ltd / Alamy Stock Photo

still a milestone. Since then the group has released another three albums, albeit at a slower pace of roughly one every five years, and are now seen as a heritage act. The three songwriters take their time and still share their duties across albums, while the band tour the globe to devotees far and wide whenever they choose. Most recent album release *Here* went to number ten in 2016 and shows the unadulterated love the band still commands today.

With a debut release on a flexi-disc through bassist Sushil K Dade's *Pure Popcorn* fanzine, followed by a flurry of successful indie singles on Bristol's The Subway Organisation, The Soup Dragons surfaced in the mid-'80s and charted at home and abroad. Named after a character in BBC's children's show 'The Clangers', the band was taken under the wing of Big Life Management and signed fleetingly to American label Sire for their eclectic debut album *This Is Our Art*. However, they would soon go indie again and radically change their sound. Like others at the time, including Manchester's Stone Roses and Happy Mondays, The Soup Dragons were seduced by acid house, hip hop and developing technology, aiming to merge dance music and rock'n'roll.

The results were fruitful for the group when second album *Lovegod* momentarily hit the zeitgeist and broke through. The album contained amped-up singles *Backwards Dog* and *Mother Universe*, displaying their blend of sequenced beats, synthetic squelch and Stooges-inspired guitars. When they transformed The Rolling Stones' *I'm Free* into a shuffling, baggy groove, complete with Jamaican MC Junior Reid chatting on top, the album went top ten and the band went stratospheric. For

The Soup Dragons, Sean Dickson, Sushil K Dade, Paul Quinn, Jim McCulloch, in Rennes, France, 1990

Martyn Goodacre / Getty Images

the next five years the band trotted the globe, scored a US hit in *Divine Thing* and released two more albums *Hotwired* and *Hydrophonic*. Never quite living up to the runaway success of *I'm Free*, they eventually disbanded, with members making music under different guises. Songwriter Sean Dickson formed The High Fidelity and is now a DJ/producer known as Hifi Sean; Jim McCulloch played with Superstar, Green Peppers and Snowgoose; second drummer Paul Quinn joined Teenage Fanclub; and original drummer Ross Sinclair is an artist. Sushil K Dade is now known as the dub-loving Future Pilot AKA, and is a respected BBC radio producer.

After two ineffective albums and a move to Brighton, Primal Scream could well have ended up a lost cause were it not for their continual ability to connect with their own cultural surroundings. Recognising rave culture as a new awakening in pop, the band visited clubs with Alan McGee and submerged themselves in this new electronic soundtrack. Their epiphany came when DJ/producer Andrew Weatherall remixed a track *I'm Losing More Than I'll Ever Have*, completely transforming it into the dance-floor destroyer *Loaded*. With a brass fanfare, piano refrain and lolloping drum loop complete with film samples, it immediately captured a perfect moment in pop. Now regarded as a defining club anthem, *Loaded* paved the way for *Come Together*, *Higher Than The Sun* and *Don't Fight It, Feel It* – all barely disguised paeans to the new sense of community within the rave scene. With full-time keyboard player Martin Duffy, their third album *Screamadelica* combined these singles and gospel-tinged *Moving On Up* into an expansive work that brought dub, house, ambience, country and rock music all under one roof. It was a crucial album for a new generation and went on to win the inaugural Mercury Music Prize in 1992. Primal Scream had finally arrived and brought with them some genuinely innovative and exploratory music.

Never ones to repeat themselves their next move was to make a classic rock'n'-roll album owing more to The Rolling Stones than house music. The critics may not have warmed to *Give Out But Don't Give Up,* but it was loved by the fans who sent the single *Rocks* into the top ten. After a heavy touring schedule and a notorious reputation for narcotics and alcohol, Primal Scream soon disappeared and nursed their wounds with rumours of a split. They would return, however, with a new bassist

Gary 'Mani' Mounfield of The Stone Roses and an album *Vanishing Point*, further exploring their interest in dub with Weatherall at the helm once again. They also nurtured a relationship with notorious Edinburgh author Irvine Welsh around this time, making a single together and including their own song *Trainspotting* on the newly-released soundtrack for the film based on his novel. Despite drug problems, line-up instabilities and the occasional mauling by the media, the Scream always seemed to be in the right place at the right time. Group talisman Bobby Gillespie also managed to tap into the hippest parts of his own record collection if required, reinventing the group from album to album.

Their best work in a decade would appear next as *XTRMNTR*, seeing My Bloody Valentine guitar-wizard Kevin Shields join the band alongside guest appearances from The Chemical Brothers and Bernard Sumner of New Order. It would be their noisiest, most uncompromising music yet, with punk, techno and German *kosmische* music all absorbed into the sound. The results were confrontational but satisfying, with single *Swastika Eyes* going to number twenty-two and the album to number

Primal Scream, with Bobby Gillespie
(second, right), behind the WEA offices in
London, 1987

Stephen Parker / Alamy Stock Photo

three in 2000. Primal Scream have continued to startle and amaze with each release since, offering up hit albums and appearing as an increasingly reliable live band and festival headliner. Over the 2000s to date they have released another five albums with the core of Gillespie, Andrew Innes and Martin Duffy in the band. After a twentieth anniversary tour of the genre-busting *Screamadelica*, Mani left in 2011 to rejoin The Stone Roses, and sadly Robert 'Throb' Young passed away in 2014. Despite this, the band's light has remained undiminished and their most recent album *Chaosmosis* sounds as fresh as ever. Viva la Scream!

Much like its high-profile indie bands, Scotland's club scene also flourished in the '90s. Edinburgh's The Venue housed the night 'UFO', which would soon morph into the legendary 'Pure' to become one of the UK's most essential platforms for cutting-edge house, techno and eclectic electronica. Run by local DJs JD Twitch and Brainstorm, 'Pure' booked mythic American DJs such as Jeff Mills, Derrick May and Joey Beltram, as well as the cream of European talent and Scottish alt-rave mainstay Ege Bam Yasi. It was rumoured to be the 'maddest' night in Scotland for almost a decade, as pill-popping locals rubbed shoulders with loved-up football casuals and thrill-seekers from across the land. Other respected local nights included 'Sativa' and 'Tribal Funktion', with Edinburgh acknowledged as Scotland's club capital.

Out west, Glasgow had the Sub Club which opened its doors in 1987 and is now known as the longest running dance club in the world. It is constantly voted as one of the top-ten places to dance in various polls, and also has an immaculate local reputation. It came into its own in the '90s with the regular 'Subculture' nights hosted by regulars Harri and Domenic, and the installation of a massive 'bodysonic' dance-floor in the 2000s that reinvented the club experience for the city. JD Twitch's post-'Pure' adventure saw him move to Glasgow and team up with JG Wilkes on new night 'Optimo'. This also bolstered the Sub Club's status, with 'Optimo' proving to be one of the most visionary clubnights on earth. Running from 1997–2010, 'Optimo' attracted a ton of world-class, genre-mashing guest DJs, as well as live acts including Franz Ferdinand, LCD Soundsystem and Hot Chip.

Intertwined with the history of the Sub Club is Glasgow duo Stuart McMillan and Orde Meikle, house connoisseurs better known as Slam. Starting life DJ-ing in

1988, they have gone on to greater things since. Realising the strength in owning their own rights and controlling distribution within the dance scene, they set up their label Soma Records in 1991 with co-manager Dave Clarke, which runs successfully to this day. As well as their own Slam releases, including the pioneering *Positive Education* which scraped the top forty in 1995, Soma is also famous for helping an array of international artists. *Da Funk* came out on vinyl via the label in 1995 and marked the beginning of a remarkable career for Daft Punk. Other key records came from One Dove, Funk D'Void and Jeff Mills, and the label retains its position as an important UK techno stable. Well connected and ambitious, Slam became more famous for hosting an extraordinary line-up of acts each year at 'T in the Park' in their very own Slam Tent.

If Slam, 'Pure' and 'Optimo' showed off the cooler, credible side of club culture in Scotland, then a more populist approach was also catered for at the massive 'Rezerection' and 'Fantazia' nights held in fields and sports arenas. Although DJs were flown in from afar, the best known local act from that scene was probably The Time Frequency. Brainchild of Jon Campbell in 1990, their hey-day came soon after when they scored a number-eight hit single with *Real Love 93* featuring Mary Kiani on vocals. Still a going concern, they have released two albums, various singles and are currently working on new material. Other contemporary ravers of the time were Ayrshire crew Ultra-Sonic, who joined forces in 1991. The band went on to sell over 300,000 records, tour the world and win a selection of awards. Main-man Mallorca Lee would work with another Ayrshire band at the end of the '90s, Public Domain, putting the *Operation Blade (Bass In The Place)* single on the UK number-five spot, famously sampling Public Enemy and New Order. Lee is now a renowned DJ specialising in trance and hard house music, but many of his shows are nostalgic sets harking back to the scene in 1994 and playing out his past glories. For many a sweaty raver, these groups are the soundtrack to their long-lost youth.

While the Bellshill scene was ploughing its furrow, grunge-apologists Stiltskin had a chart-topping single *Inside* and techno was waking up club culture. Another wave of independent labels was cropping up within Glasgow's thriving DIY scene too. Taking influence from Creation and Postcard Records, Chemikal Underground was

founded in 1994 out of necessity more than anything else. Grabbing hold of their own destiny, Glasgow-based indie rockers The Delgados set up the endeavour simply as a home for their own music. The single *Monica Webster* was the band and label's debut and caught the attention of John Peel who would champion the group across many BBC radio sessions from then onwards. Never a band to trouble the mainstream, or in fact realise their true commercial potential, they did put out five excellent albums and have a big cultural impact on Scotland. Named after Spanish cyclist Pedro Delgado, first album *Domestiques* was largely the sound of noisy guitars, youthful vim and vigour; follow-up *Peloton* showed their burgeoning ambition. These artistic aspirations were fully realised on the swirling epic single *The Great Eastern* produced by American sonic alchemist Dave Fridmann and released in 2000. With key singles grazing the charts, the album's depth and scale showed a group unafraid to blend orchestral strings, loud guitars and cerebral song-craft. It would become a serious influence on future Scottish indie kids and was lauded at the time by *MOJO* magazine among others of the music press. Two more superb albums, *Hate*

Stiltskin, January 1994

Erica Echenberg / Getty Images

and *Universal Audio*, were released to further acclaim, but The Delgados would regrettably call an end to their career in 2005, blighted by commercial indifference.

The Delgados boasted two accomplished songwriters – Emma Pollock, who has blossomed as an exceptional solo artist over a series of impressive albums, and Alun Woodward who intermittently records under the pseudonym Lord Cut Glass. Finally tiring of the music industry, bassist Stewart Henderson is now a fireman, but drummer Paul Savage has built up a reputation as a respected record producer. Perhaps the group's greatest legacy is that of their label and recording studio. Chemikal Underground has existed since 1994, promoting crucial recordings by over thirty different groups from Scotland and elsewhere over almost twenty-five years. These included famously initiating successful careers for Mogwai and Arab Strap. Their Blantyre-based recording studio Chem19, helmed by Savage, is regarded as one of the finest in the country with artists flocking from all over the UK to work there. Remaining in Scotland rather than fleeing to London also showed courage, demonstrating to future musicians the possibilities of doing things on their own terms. Most Scottish musicians now keep their base north of the border and connect with London only for necessary business.

Chemikal Underground's first dalliance with success came, incredibly, with only their second ever release. Bis was a teenage trio from Glasgow who mixed the jerky new wave of Devo, the eight-bit electro of primitive synth-pop and 'C86' indie's 'twee' aesthetics into a punky, animated whole. Chemikal released their debut *Secret Vampire Soundtrack* EP, with single *Kandy Pop* securing them an appearance on 'Top of the Pops'. This was a real coup as Bis were fledgling and unsigned. After the resulting publicity the band were central to an industry bidding-war, but faithfully stayed independent in the UK on the Wiiija label while signing to Beastie Boys' Grand Royal outlet in the States. With effervescent energy, Riot Grrrl politics and a hand-drawn cartoon aesthetic, the band's artistic reach probably surpassed their commercial one. In the late '90s, walking the streets of hipster enclaves in the UK, USA and Europe, you could see Manda Rin, Sci-Fi Steven and John Disco lookalikes everywhere. Japan took the band to heart as well, putting their debut album *The New Transistor Heroes* into the Japanese top twenty. At home though, their commercial ambitions were somewhat hampered. Despite touring far and wide, soundtracking children's television shows, releasing two more albums, *Social Dancing* and *Return To Central*, and building a genuine cult following worldwide, the group separated in 2003. Alongside solo works and side-projects, Bis decided to re-form in 2009 and released fourth album *Data Panik Etcetera* in 2014. Their fifth is due soon.

Who would think that one of Scotland's most enduring acts would be an effects-pedal driven guitar band that played largely instrumental pieces? Mogwai took an utterly uncompromising approach to studio and live work from the start, becoming local legends in Scotland and establishing the band as a surprising global phenomenon. Today they perform to thousands across Europe, Asia and the USA, the critics adore them and their dedicated fanbase commits to every release. They must be one of Scotland's most successful musical exports in years.

Formed in 1995, Mogwai signed to Chemikal Underground and immediately gained the patronage of John Peel. Sonically they haven't deviated too far from their initial formula over the decades, with a love of The Cure, My Bloody Valentine and Slint on display throughout lengthy and emotional musical passages. Their trademark sound counterbalances bludgeoning, heavy riffola with twinkling, ethereal guitar lines, piano, electronica and strings, and they have had occasional vocal contributions from guests as well as the individual band members.

Initial mission statement *Mogwai Young Team* in 1997 turned heads and made a point, before the second album *Come On Die Young* (1999) cemented their name in indie folklore by reaching the top thirty. Third album *Rock Action*, called after Stooges drummer Scott Asheton, went to number twenty-three and gave them the name of their own record label through which they release music today. By the year 2000 Mogwai had proved they were here to stay. To date they have released nine studio albums, as well as countless singles, EPs, compilations and live recordings. Their 2014 album *Rave Tapes* hit number ten in the charts, and the recent *Every Country's Son* went even higher in 2017. Rather than exploding, burning brightly and then petering out, against all the odds Mogwai have seen their music grow in popularity and professionalism. The albums sell in increasing numbers and their deafening live show attracts more kudos year-on-year. Mogwai are now often considered within the

realms of so-called 'high art' and invited to play at concert halls and arts festivals. Having soundtracked the documentaries 'Zidane – a 21st Century Portrait' and Mark Cousins' 'Atomic – Living in Dread and Promise', as well as French television drama 'Les Revenants', they have also contributed music to films 'The Fountain' and 'Before the Flood', collaborating with Clint Mansell and Trent Reznor among others.

Described continually as 'post-rock', Mogwai actually play a modern form of psychedelic rock more in common with minimalist classical music than pop. Although their music is austere in tone, with loud/quiet dynamics and looming areas of space and eeriness, the band members are jovial and down-to-earth. With a cheeky and irreverent attitude to the music press in the '90s, they famously mocked their Brit-pop contemporaries and even dared to sell T-shirts at their shows with the iconic slogan, 'Blur Are Shite' – although the band have declined to print more since, becoming slightly more dignified in old age.

The band's core of Stuart Braithwaite, Dominic Aitchison, Barry Burns and Martin Bulloch continue as a unit, with long-time member John Cummings having

Mogwai, Heineken Primavera Sound
Festival, Barcelona, May 2014

Christian Bertrand / Alamy Stock Photo

left in 2015. It looks like the band will last far into the future, blowing even more minds and eardrums.

Another unlikely phenomenon is Falkirk's Arab Strap. Getting together in 1995, and forming a bond with Chemikal Underground, Malcolm Middleton and Aidan Moffat started as a recording duo before recruiting others to create a full band and accompanying sound. Moffat regaled his listeners with his poignant, world-weary, sexually-explicit spoken word over sequenced drums, sparse guitar and bass parts played by Middleton. Debut single *The First Big Weekend* became an instant cult classic when Radio 1 DJ Steve Lamacq championed it relentlessly on air. Soon Moffat's vignettes and Middleton's accompanying sonic tapestries would make it onto their debut album *The Week Never Starts Around Here* and worm their way into the hearts of listeners all over the country. Over six superb and utterly idiosyncratic albums – including *Philophobia* which went top forty, *Elephant Shoe*, *The Red Thread* and *Monday At The Hug And Pint* – the band fused rock, folk and electronic music, effortlessly constructing a new indie-rock template for Scotland alongside Mogwai

Arab Strap, with singer Aidan Moffat, at
Richard's in Vancouver, Canada,
November 2003

and The Delgados. Contemporary Scottish life, good and bad, could be heard in the grooves of these albums in a distinct vernacular not heard since The Proclaimers.

Deadpan humour, sad but beautiful music and a devoted following, couldn't stop Arab Strap from eventually laying the group to rest. After releasing a final album, fittingly called *The Last Romance*, followed by a compilation *Ten Years Of Tears*, it was goodbye in 2006. But with their reputation still growing there was an overwhelming reaction to the announcement that the band would re-form and play some live shows in 2016. The sold-out events included two phenomenal nights at the Glasgow Barrowland Ballroom. Festivals followed and it now looks as if Arab Strap may appear again from time to time. Another record? We'll see.

As these groups proved, playing uncompromising music and living in Scotland was not necessarily a hindrance to success. As a result Glasgow's DIY indie scene grew at pace with groups such as provocative post-punks The Yummy Fur and Sonic Youth-loving Urusei Yatsura. Bands were forming and connecting with the late-night John Peel radio audience and a network of indie lovers throughout the UK. Urusei Yatsura would even score a number-forty single with *Hello Tiger* in 1997. Alex Kapranos, soon to be frontman of Franz Ferdinand, helped run a night in Glasgow's The 13th Note called 'The Kazoo Club' which acted as a hub for this disparate gang of outcasts and gave musicians the chance to experiment with new sounds and songs. Other like-minded groups from around Scotland, born in the '90s, were building an audience too, such as Dundee's Spare Snare who would go on to enjoy four sessions for John Peel and release a catalogue of albums on their own Chute label. The UK was waking up to another Scottish scene that was expanding way beyond its meagre confines.

One band who would make an extremely significant impression was Belle & Sebastian. Based in Glasgow's West End and named after a French novel *Belle et Sébastien* by Cécile Aubry (and children's TV series), the project came to life slowly as the songwriting vehicle for Stuart Murdoch. By 1996 they had developed into a full band featuring Stuart David, Stevie Jackson, Isobel Campbell and Richard Colburn. Murdoch's winsome, fragile delivery, combined with his intimate, storytelling lyrics, chimed with local indie kids immediately. Those in love with 'C86', Felt, Love and The Velvet Underground had a new hero. A debut album *Tigermilk* was recorded and

released through Stow College's Electric Honey student label and limited to one thousand copies – considered gold dust today. Shy, anti-macho, uncompromising and non-corporate in outlook, the band refused to do most press interviews and even to appear in public at first. It would be a while before they began to tour and play for their growing army of stripey-topped, bowl-cut aficionados. Rather than being commercial suicide, however, this only helped to build the almost cultish devotion to the band. Indeed Belle & Sebastian would soon be likened to The Smiths for the 1990s.

The group's next album *If You're Feeling Sinister* (1997) would prove to be their masterpiece. Understated but exact, with a depth and sincerity rarely heard in pop, bookish outsiders and super-fans return to the work over and over. Even Murdoch considers it his finest collection. From the artwork to the melodies and those all-important lyrics, the album captures the essence of Murdoch's wit and melancholy, crystallising his vision. Over their continuing twenty-plus year career, the group has gone on to release nine full studio albums, numerous EPs and singles via Jeepster, Rough Trade and Matador Records, with a growing proficiency and hooks aplenty.

Belle & Sebastian, Austin City Limits Music Festival, Texas, USA, 2014

© Daniel DeSlover / ZUMA Wire / Alamy Live News

They've won a Brit award, appeared on 'Top of the Pops', recorded with Trevor Horn, scored top-ten albums, headlined the Hollywood Bowl, toured the globe and unwittingly wrestled the mantle from BMX Bandits to perhaps becoming the ultimate indie-pop band. Although others in the group contribute to songwriting and singing lead vocals across their extensive back catalogue, Murdoch is still seen as the band-leader and is an unusual character, openly religious in the secular world of rock.

Nowadays the band interact with press and have become veritable festival headliners with a slick live show and level of musicianship at odds with their amateur beginnings. Belle & Sebastian's line-up may have changed here and there, but they are now firmly on the world stage and seem more comfortable than ever in their own skin. Never flashy or over-confident, they have quietly conquered the world.

If Glasgow's underground guitar scene was buoyant and bubbling, the rest of Scotland was more subdued and attracted less coverage. Edinburgh had to have its say though, and Idlewild soon put the city back on the map. Singer Roddy Woomble, guitarist Rod Jones and drummer Colin Newton have been the group's core since its formation in 1995, with bass-players and extra musicians coming and going through the ranks. Their first outing was the bratty single *Queen Of The Troubled Teens*. It did its job though, grabbing the attention of Steve Lamacq and Radio 1's Evening Session. Soon signed to the Deceptive label, the band improved dramatically on the thrashy *Captain* mini-album, much loved by long-term fans. Sonically Idlewild were distorted, discordant and more overtly grunge-influenced than many of their Glasgow counterparts, but slowly began to develop their songwriting skills as the influence of The Smiths and REM crept into their sound. Moving to the Parlophone imprint Food Records saw them capitalise on their indie kudos and propel them further towards the genuine mainstream rock market. The momentum was with them and second album *Hope Is Important* (1998) displayed their ongoing potential, with single *When I Argue I See Shapes* cracking the top twenty.

Third album *100 Broken Windows* (2000) is now seen as a benchmark in Scottish rock and was voted 'Best Album of the Decade' by *The Skinny* magazine. It was also something of a watershed for the band, who were audibly moving away from their punkier roots towards a more measured songwriting approach. The balance

between the post-punk guitars and the maturing vocal hooks was just right, with all the album's singles denting the top forty. However, with the following album *The Remote Part* they would experience their finest commercial hour. Woomble would further explore literary fascinations and poetry, collaborating with the Makar poet Edwin Morgan. Their biggest hit was the number-nine single *You Held The World In Your Arms* and the album became their most recognised to date. With support slots to Pearl Jam, The Rolling Stones and their beloved REM, the band were on their way to becoming a globally renowned act. Rock'n'roll is a funny old game though, and there are no such things as certainties. In another world Idlewild could have become stadium fillers, but they had in fact plateaued in terms of popularity. But with the final album *Warnings/Promises* for Parlophone in 2005 and a succession of independent released albums since, the band have established themselves as mainstays to their fans and on the festival circuit. Idlewild showed they still had something to prove when, after a brief hiatus, their self-released album *Everything*

Idlewild, Edinburgh's Hogmanay Concert,
Princes Street Gardens, 2015/16

Brian Wilson / Alamy News Live

Ever Written (2015) went into the top twenty. Woomble has also enjoyed a celebrated folk-inspired solo career and Jones has set up the Post Electric recording studio in Leith, Edinburgh. They're certainly not done yet.

Despite a vibrant local scene at The Venue, Cas Rock and Subway, Edinburgh had actually become more synonymous with club culture, techno, reggae and hip hop. Although the nightlife was jumping at venues such as Café Graffiti, The Bongo Club and La Belle Angele, there were few successes in terms of original groups. The Chimes had a single hit with their soulful version of U2's *I Still Haven't Found What I'm Looking For*, Sugar Bullet promised a lot but fell by the wayside, and the East Coast Project showcased the city's hip-hop scene with support from the Stereo MCs. The door was opened but few managed to walk through – until, that is, a certain Finlay Quaye stepped up and signed to a major label in 1994. Quaye had it all on a plate when debut album *Maverick A Strike* made a massive breakthrough in 1997. His radio-friendly mixture of reggae, hip hop, pop and rock saw the platinum album produce hit singles *Sunday Shining* and *Even After All*, and win Brit and MOBO awards. Quaye and his band toured the globe to plaudits from the critics before he famously embarked on celebrity relationships and a personal downward spiral. Signed to Epic he would go on to release two more albums for the label, albeit to diminishing returns. Despite all this, Finlay Quaye was and is a serious talent and his star lit up the UK music scene in the late 1990s.

In timely fashion, a group materialised at the Edinburgh College of Art who managed to blend the disparate genres of rock'n'roll, hip hop, house and acoustic folk into one psychedelic melting-pot. Inspired by Primal Scream, The KLF, Beck and the cut'n'paste medium of visual and audio collage, The Beta Band relocated to London and were signed to EMI through the Regal imprint, thanks to a four-track demo-cassette passing from hand to hand. After founding member Gordon Anderson left for health reasons, the group comprised two Fifers Steve Mason and John Maclean, alongside Edinburgh drummer Robin Jones and Londoner Richard Greentree. A refreshing change from the clattering noise of indie rock and the clichéd repetition of dance music, The Beta Band injected a sense of freedom, abandonment and surrealist humour into proceedings. From their recording techniques to their press photographs, via self-filmed videos and homespun artwork, the band distanced themselves from the banalities of the music business and laughed from afar at the corniness inherent in the whole operation. The Beta Band reminded their audience of a hip-hop Beatles, often dressed as Mexican bandits or astronauts – plus they had catchy tunes. But unlike The Beatles their record sales did not skyrocket. Instead, more like The Velvet Underground, the band inspired everyone who saw them.

Their opening EP *Champion Versions* catapulted the band into the limelight as they became the improbable poster-boys for the music press and were universally praised by other musicians. Subsequent releases *The Patty Patty Sound* and *Los Amigos Del Beta Bandidos* were also applauded and soon collected on the now timeless *3 EPs* compilation, building anticipation for a bright future. Ever the contrarians though, the group recorded a hugely expensive but commercially disastrous self-titled debut album. Disjointed and experimental, it has become a real curio to fans and is a pleasantly eccentric listen, though it was released to a critical backlash and even slated by Steve Mason himself. A more concise second album with sniggering title *Hotshots II* regained some ground as they toured with Radiohead in America. Their swansong would come with the third album, the self-deprecating *Heroes To Zeroes* in 2004, before the band called it quits.

Not only name-checked in the Hollywood film 'High Fidelity', all three of their studio albums went into the top twenty and The Beta Band's lasting inspiration spread across the globe into various nooks and crannies. Wilfully at odds with the music industry, they would turn down a one million dollar advertising contract, offend countless journalists, get bumped from a 'Top of the Pops' appearance, and even threaten a US president from the stage. They were mavericks in so many ways, but also suffered at the hands of some accountants and managers. After their demise, Anderson was reunited with Maclean and Jones in The Aliens, and Steve Mason continues to enjoy a successful solo career under his own name and various pseudonyms. There are rumours that the original band will re-form one day, but as John Maclean is now the respected film director of 'Slow West', it is doubtful when that will actually happen.

Edinburgh's Shirley Manson served her musical apprenticeship in the '80s and early '90s as keyboard-player and backing vocalist for Goodbye Mr Mackenzie. But when she began to front the reworked version of the band renamed Angelfish, she was noticed on MTV by American music producer Steve Marker and invited to join a new band with fellow producers Butch Vig and Duke Erikson. Manson accepted and the group in question were delightfully christened Garbage. They set out to mix industrial, alternative rock with acerbic new wave and pop, and were very successful from the off. Manson would not only become one of Scotland's most instantly recognisable singers, but a global ambassador for fearsome front-women. Singles *Stupid Girl* and *Only Happy When It Rains* became alt-rock staples and Manson immediately became a role-model.

Garbage has now sold in excess of twelve million albums, been nominated for Grammy awards, recorded a James Bond film theme and toured the globe countless times. After a run of four albums from 1995–2005, the band enjoyed a long hiatus before returning with new material and their own record label in 2012. Since then

The Beta Band, with Steve Mason, at the
Fridge, Brixton, London, 2001

Martyn Goodacre / Getty Images

Garbage has been operational, recording albums and performing live. Although based in America, Manson remains fiercely proud of her Scottish roots and the group always plays key concerts in the country as part of their global tour schedule. In 1999, after the Labour Government sanctioned the vote on Devolution and Scotland was granted its own Parliament, Garbage headlined the spectacular celebration in the Ross Bandstand in Edinburgh's Princes Street Gardens.

As relative political and financial stability reigned throughout the UK during the 1990s and Britpop brought new confidence to homegrown rock and pop, Scotland's music flourished with both mainstream triumphs and under-the-radar scenesters. The country was becoming a music destination in its own right. And with a proven track-record through yet another decade, as the new millennium arrived Scotland had belief in its own modern national identity. The next wave of Scottish pop was waiting around the corner, and astonishingly its biggest achievements were yet to come.

Garbage, with Shirley Manson, *c.1996*

Chapter nine
Take me out

At the turn of the new millennium, with the Devolution Referendum in 1997 leading to the establishment of its own Parliament, Scotland's two most successful decades of popular music were about to begin. From indie guitar bands, through singer-songwriters, to world-beating electronic producers, the country would prove it could punch well above its weight and demonstrate how local could become global. Soon certain artists would exceed even the achievements of those in the 1980s. A homespun music industry had also emerged and an infrastructure of record labels, live venues, print and digital media, as well as a dedicated local audience, were thriving. The national rock and pop festival 'T in the Park' was growing in stature and audience numbers, becoming second only to Glastonbury in size within the United Kingdom.

During years of more moderate, centrist UK Governments and the investment they had made in the economy, Scotland began to diversify and appeared more outward-looking than ever. Although London's pull remained strong, musicians and those in the creative industries were increasingly inclined to keep their headquarters in Scotland. Record and ticket-buying audiences were more accepting and supportive of homegrown acts, regardless of whether they made it in London or not. Irvine Welsh's 'Trainspotting' film in the late '90s, based around a group of feckless Edinburgh junkies, was also hugely important and became the hippest thing in town, with a radical soundtrack in tow. And after fifteen years of Devolution, there would even be an Independence Referendum in 2014 as a new political, economic and social confidence flourished.

Good things come to those who wait – and one band who put in years of hard work to a deafening silence were Glasgow rockers Travis. Slogging it on Scotland's 'toilet circuit' during the '90s under the name of Glass Onion, they had attempted to woo London record companies for years, but the whole experience was demoralising and fruitless. With a change of name, steadfast work ethic and the obvious talent of singer-songwriter Fran Healy, the band decided to have one last crack at it. Thanks

Pages 154–55: Fireworks over Edinburgh, 2014

Shahid Khan / Shutterstock.com

to a long-time supporter, they signed a modest deal with Sony Music Publishing and moved to London. Travis would be one of the last few Scottish acts of repute to go there, but it was the right thing to do. Toughening up their trademark sound on tracks such as *All I Want To Do Is Rock*, the debut album *Good Feeling* was crafted in the States and released on the Independiente label. Other standout songs such as *Tied To The '90s* and *Happy* saw the album ride in on the coat-tails of Britpop and catch the attention of Noel Gallagher and others. The band's passion and no-nonsense approach chimed with audiences and their debut album went top ten, a great achievement for a band considered almost washed-up. Instead, their real glory days were just ahead.

Travis' style of heartfelt, melodic rock, centred on Healy's soaring vocals, would develop into something of a prototype for the next wave of up-and-coming bands such as Coldplay and Keane. On their second album, *The Man Who* (1999), the group broke the glass ceiling and became a household name, due in part to the anthemic single *Why Does It Always Rain On Me?* Here was a simple, timeless song that seemed tailor-made for UK audiences, developing into a ubiquitous summer festival sing-along when the inevitable happened. Less rugged and rocking than their debut album, *The Man Who* enjoyed a lengthy lifespan and eventually hit the number-one spot. It sat there for over two months, housing other singles such as *Turn* and *Drift-wood*. This proved to be a game-changer for the band and saw yet another Caledonian indie rock outfit go multi-platinum, headline festivals and tour the world. Travis would then repeat the trick with third album *The Invisible Band* (2001), showing their love of songwriting and indifference to fame. Healy would often talk

Fran Healy of Travis at the 'T in the Park' music festival, 1999

Jeremy Sutton-Hibbert / Alamy Stock Photo

about the power of the songs and how they were more famous than the band itself, hence the album title. *Side, Sing* and *Flowers In The Window* all proved to be massive hits and the band's multi-million-selling stock had never been higher.

The group were then forced into a temporary hiatus when the drummer Neil Primrose broke his neck after miscalculating a dive into a swimming-pool. Mercifully he made a full recovery and Travis was able to record and tour again. A darker more contemplative fourth album, *12 Memories* (2003), went to number three but saw the band's popularity plateau. They would never quite reach the dizzying heights of the previous albums, but had established themselves within the mainstream music community and become dependable purveyors of quality. In Scotland the band is rightfully lauded as one of the country's greatest, which must instil some satisfaction when they look back to those early years of struggle. To date Travis has released eight studio albums, the last of which *Everything At Once* went to number five in the UK charts and showed that their support has not diminished. With Brit awards and performances across the world alongside the biggest and best, the band are true ambassadors for Scotland. Long may they continue to rock.

Another band to play the long game was Snow Patrol. Centred on Northern Irish friends Gary Lightbody and Mark McClelland, they formed at the University of Dundee in 1994 before moving to Glasgow to become mainstays of the vibrant scene centred on legendary nightspot NiceNSleazy. With a sound influenced by alt-American acts such as Sebadoh, they collaborated with student label Electric Honey on their *Starfighter Pilot* EP before signing to the Jeepster label, also home to friends Belle & Sebastian. The band underwent a line-up change, adding long-standing drummer and business brain Jonny Quinn, then set out on a period of constant touring with the release of two critically acclaimed but commercially unsuccessful albums. The group were well-loved in Scotland and Northern Ireland by a small but dedicated fanbase, but financially were on their hunkers and seriously needed a break. As relief from their increasingly grim existence, Lightbody coalesced a collection of movers and shakers from Glasgow to form The Reindeer Section. Members of Mogwai, Arab Strap, Belle & Sebastian, Idlewild, Teenage Fanclub, The Vaselines and Astrid all took part and graced the recordings of two largely acoustic-led albums and

live appearances. It was the perfect stop-gap, a great networking exercise and served to showcase more of Lightbody's simple, emotive songwriting.

This wasn't the end of Snow Patrol, however. Far from it. Their rags-to-riches tale is a lesson in perseverance for other musicians to heed. As The Reindeer Section worked its understated magic, Snow Patrol signed with new management and Lightbody wrote a clutch of songs that would see the light of day on the aptly named third album *Final Straw* (2003). Through a music business associate from Dundee, they were signed to the Fiction/Polydor label and given a new lease of life. Expectations would be massively exceeded when the single *Run* was released and crashed into the top ten. Tirelessly championed by Radio 1 DJ friends Zane Lowe and Colin Murray, the song would become almost a modern-day hymn for festival-goers and radically transformed the band's fortunes. Now they were making 'The Big Music' beloved of stadia across the world. *Final Straw* would end up selling millions and go multi-platinum, as producer Jacknife Lee embellished their indie sound to up the rock ante. Tasting major success, the group followed it with an even more successful album, *Eyes*

Snow Patrol, (left to right) Tom Simpson, Jonny Quinn, Gary Lightbody, Nathan Connolly and Mark McClelland, at the Lighthouse, Glasgow

Trinity Mirror / Mirrorpix / Alamy Stock Photo

Open, spawning the single *Chasing Cars* which would become a global smash. Both the album and single were the biggest UK sellers in 2006 and also broke the band Stateside. Since then Snow Patrol has relocated to America and augmented the line-up to include Paul Wilson and Nathan Connolly, seeing founding bassist McClelland leave after *Final Straw*. They can now consider themselves one of the biggest acts in the world, with a seventh album *Wildness* in 2018, millions of sales, tours with U2 and Coldplay, as well as countless festival headline slots. They may be Irish-born and America-based, but they were definitely Scottish bred.

While Scotland's scene fragmented across different styles, Glasgow would constantly prove itself to be the epicentre with pockets of underground innovation. One instigator, Alex Huntley, who ran the now infamous 'Kazoo Club' at the 13th Note venue, was responsible for helping to develop some of the artier elements of the city's underbelly. Forming his own band The Blisters, who would in time be renamed The Karelia, he also played with Ska-lovers The Amphetameanies and local refusniks The Yummy Fur. Huntley would eventually rise to prominence in a dramatic way as lead-singer, guitarist and songwriter Alex Kapranos, using his father's original Greek surname. After years of learning his craft and struggling to make ends meet, his moment in the sun was about to happen.

By 2002, in the wake of a rekindled passion for art rock by The Strokes, White Stripes and Yeah Yeah Yeahs, the UK needed acts to stand alongside the Americans. Those willing to take up the challenge were waiting in the wings – step up Franz Ferdinand. Naming their ensemble after the assassinated Austro-Hungarian Arch-duke, Alex Kapranos, Bob Hardy, Paul Thomson and Nick McCarthy came together from a scene of artists, oddballs and outcasts, and concentrated on making their own fun and starting parties. Reclaiming an old, abandoned building in Glasgow – re-naming it The Chateau – they would house their shows, performing to fashion-istas and fellow musicians away from the glare of industry attention. Inevitably the word spread and London's Domino Records came knocking. With an impeccable release profile and connections throughout the indie underground they were perfect for Franz, even as the majors came sniffing. Legend has it Domino boss Laurence Bell re-mortgaged his own house to stump up the cash for the band's initial advance.

With art-school kudos, an indie powerhouse label and media momentum be-hind them, Franz Ferdinand would hit the ground running and not pause for breath until the end of the decade. The second single *Take Me Out* (January 2004) saw the band unexpectedly barge their way into the top ten, going to number three. This unusual song started fast but slowed down to mid-tempo disco groove, with the guitar riffs as catchy as the vocal hooks. Yes its roots were in post-punk, but it also pointed to the future, momentarily reinventing guitar music for a new generation. Their self-titled debut album would also land at number three in the charts, go on to win the Mercury Music Prize, and see the band tour the globe constantly for the next two years. Franz Ferdinand hadn't just hit the zeitgeist, they *were* the zeitgeist!

The world's media fell in love with the group's angular art pop, sharp threads and fine cheekbones. Polite, precise and with a singular commitment, Kapranos was now achieving his teenage dreams and complacency was not going to get in the way. Despite a hectic tour schedule, second album *You Could Have It So Much Better* (2005) capitalised on the group's runaway success, claiming a top-ten spot. With the

Franz Ferdinand, with Nick McCarthy (left) and Alex Kapranos (right), at Vega, Copenhagen, 2009

Gonzales Photo / Alamy Stock Photo

likes of Mogwai and Belle & Sebastian, they were now poster-boys for Glasgow's DIY indie scene, albeit with gigantic sales and a global profile.

Since their meteoric rise Franz Ferdinand haven't let up. Gaps between releases may have lengthened, but their craftsmanship and professionalism have continued at pace across albums *Tonight: Franz Ferdinand* (2009) and *Right Thoughts, Right Words, Right Action* (2013). An as an extraordinary curveball they co-wrote an album with Los Angeles art-glam eccentrics Sparks, under the acronym FFS, with the music and live shows joyously mixing equal amounts of quirky humour and inspired melody. Although fashion may have moved on, Franz Ferdinand is still a major draw in the UK, Europe, USA, Australasia and South America in particular. They have Brit, Ivor Novello, Q, MTV and Meteor wins in the bag, and a Grammy nomination. With an augmented line-up that includes Julian Corrie and Dino Bardot, after McCarthy's amicable exit in 2016, and a new dance-infused album *Always Ascending* in 2018, their lust for life endures and Kapranos seems more energised than ever. Still grounded in Scotland, they are one its most distinguished artistic exports.

Scotland has always been a hotbed for songwriters with an instinctive knack for melodic storytelling. Through the decades from the 1950s to the present there has been a surplus of talent willing to strap on a guitar and give us a song. As the 2000s took hold a few would take that philosophy to the very top, while others would reinvent it as a genuinely alternative lifestyle choice. The East Neuk of Fife may not seem like a veritable hub of rock'n'roll, but thanks to the cosmopolitan nature of its capital St Andrews, nearby city of discovery Dundee, and the impact of local-boys-done-good The Beta Band, that reputation would change.

KT Tunstall is the Kingdom of Fife's most famous daughter in this regard, having scaled the vertiginous heights of pop's Everest and peeked over the top. It certainly wasn't an easy ascent. Growing up in a family household without music, she discovered her own innate abilities and honed her craft through busking locally and during a school away-year in Kent, Connecticut, USA. Also important was meeting the Anderson brothers in St Andrews. They would inspire her ideas, attitude and deft musicianship, and also have musical careers of their own.

After years of toil, false starts and misguided potential in the '90s, Tunstall's first proper foot on the ladder was a modest deal with Relentless Records in 2003. Like Travis, Scotland was not initially receptive to her music, so she made the time-honoured move to London to study music and drama. Her debut album *Eye To The Telescope* was released in 2004 to muted applause, but a breakthrough was on its way thanks to television exposure on BBC2's 'Later … with Jools Holland'. When rapper Nas had to cancel, a space was offered to the twenty-nine-year-old. Armed with only a guitar and loop pedal she performed a new song not included on the album at the request of her label. *Black Horse And The Cherry Tree*, with its country-blues inflections and addictive 'woo-hoo' refrain, performed by this soulful one-woman band, floored the studio and home audience alike. Right place, right time and KT Tunstall with her undeniable talent was on her way.

Tailor-made for radio, Tunstall's songs won a mainstream audience with *Black Horse*, one of the most played songs of the year and henceforth included on the album which flew up the charts. Future singles helped her rising profile, with *Suddenly I See* cracking the US charts and appearing in the soundtrack of the film 'The Devil Wears Prada'. Over three years Tunstall slowly but surely conquered the world, always affable and unflappable. From unknown Fifer to global star she put in a serious shift touring relentlessly across as many continents as possible.

Like Alex Kapranos, this was Tunstall's childhood dream and she wanted it to work out long-term. With the release of the successful follow-up *Drastic Fantastic* (2007) and three more albums since, her dream was realised. She has won Ivor Novello and Brit awards, while standing up for fellow female artists and raising aware-

KT Tunstall

Zoonar GmbH / Alamy Stock Photo

ness about climate change. A genuine force of nature herself, she has more recently studied screen composition and proven to be a world-class songwriter for television and film, as well as selling many millions of albums. Always up for a challenge, she has collaborated with artists as diverse as Travis, Suzanne Vega and Howe Gelb, taking busking and her own song-craft to new levels.

Music was in the blood of the aforementioned Anderson brothers, with their father an accordionist, Scottish country dance band-leader and radio presenter. The eldest, Kenny, is now better known under his pseudonym King Creosote and, much like KT Tunstall, took the long way round to success. After a foray into 1980s pop at the University of Glasgow, his first real group was a motley crew who formed as an ever-evolving busking band, mixing skiffle, blue-grass and folk into an unruly concoction. Naming themselves Skoubhie Dubh Orchestra, his brother Een would join on double bass and move to banjo as his musicianship progressed. Their reputation as a wild, breakneck live act was notorious, and those enamoured by Swamptrash and We Free Kings had someone new to cherish. However, it was Kenny's melancholy ballads and his yearning, plaintive delivery that would soon be his forte. The Dubhs slowly morphed from a party band into a more serious proposition. But even after a heavy touring schedule, a selection of albums and a name-change to Khartoum Heroes, their luck ran out and Kenny retired in frustration from the music industry.

By the late '90s, back in his beloved East Neuk, Kenny continued to do the thing he loved most – home recording. Amassing a now mythical back catalogue of albums, he decided to use the technology of the day and burn the albums one-by-one onto CDs, selling them locally in St Andrews. Simultaneously he began to book live nights in the Aikman's wine bar, bringing together like-minded souls and disgruntled musicians. Taking control of the local record shop, he named it 'Fence' after the small DIY label he had set up to release his CDs, and soon the gigs also came under the same banner. His brother Een became Pip Dylan, brother Gordon became Lone Pigeon (and the frontman of The Aliens), while other local musicians adopted pseudonyms such as Uncle Beesly, HMS Ginafore and Captain Geeko the Dead Aviator. The 'Fence Collective' was born and quickly became an umbrella for songwriters, bands and outsiders from the local community. With their disregard for the 'established' music industry, they made their own fun by writing, recording and producing material in and around St Andrews and the nearby fishing villages. Riotous gigs incorporated fancy dress, comedy sketches, Scalextric tracks, baked goods from St Andrews baker Fisher & Donaldson, and lots of improvised music – not exactly polished and professional. The sense of freedom was irresistible and drew people from far and wide, eventually including Laurence Bell of Domino Records. He would sign James Yorkston from the scene before working with the Anderson brothers.

Though Kenny fervently rejected the music business, as the buzz grew around Fence the labels began to circle, noticing a collection of exceptional songwriters amid the madness. King Creosote finally allowed Domino to collaborate with Fence on albums *Kenny & Beth's Musikal Boat Rides* (2003) and *Rocket DIY* (2005), before signing to Warner Brothers offshoot 679 Records for his breakthrough albums *KC Rules OK* and *Bombshell*. The prolific contrarian enjoyed the might of a major behind him to launch his extraordinary songs onto an unsuspecting public. The key to King Creosote and Fence's success, however, was not the strangely exotic location of Fife, but the strength of the songs themselves. This was not unlistenable thrash or punk, but songs composed using acoustic guitar and voice. Away from the London media, it possessed a purity missing from most other music at that time. Soon Fence would be co-helmed by Johnny Lynch (The Pictish Trail) and a certain ambition crept into the proceedings. 'Homegame' festivals sold out in minutes and the community expanded far beyond its humble, chaotic beginnings. The East Neuk became a tourist destination for reasons other than golf and fish 'n' chips!

As King Creosote, Anderson would eventually return to Domino where he remains to this day. More albums have come thick and fast, including his two most successful ventures yet – the Mercury-nominated collaboration with Jon Hopkins, *Diamond Mine*, and the soundtrack to the astonishing archive film 'From Scotland with Love'. Both records magnified his already fanatical following, bringing in new fans. Still resolutely individualistic in nature, Anderson and The Pictish Trail have sadly parted ways, but Fence is still alive in theory as Kenny works on and off the radar with constant vinyl-only releases and local gigs. With approximately fifty albums in his archives, he is an inimitable voice in Scotland's music landscape, doggedly refusing

to capitulate to digital innovations such as streaming, and standing against Scottish Independence in the face of an almost unanimous 'Yes' voting artistic community. King Creosote is a true individual and all the more interesting for it.

As an early member of the nascent Fence Collective, under the name J. Wright Presents, James Yorkston was in fact the first songwriter to help shine an outside light on the unconventional Fife scene, specifically after his Domino signing. Like Kenny Anderson, Yorkston was utterly disenchanted with the music industry when he began to record his own acoustic music and perform as a solo act. After support slots to Bert Jansch and John Martyn and a single via the Bad Jazz label, he was able to embark on a musical career at the unlikely age of thirty, after years of disappointment in beat combos such as Miraclehead, Agapapa and Huckleberry.

With Domino's patronage, *Moving Up Country* became the debut album by James Yorkston and the Athletes and fitted perfectly with the times. It made his name in the public eye as many searched for authenticity in a sea of processed pop. Here was a record that combined the simple essence of folk and pop across some genuinely great songs at the vanguard of an acoustic renaissance. An inspiration to

King Creosote at the Greenman Festival,
Glanusk Park, Brecon Beacons, Wales,
2008

shot2bits.net_westmacott / Alamy Stock
Photo

budding songwriters, he has been highly praised by the broadsheet newspapers since and was one of the very last to record a John Peel session before the untimely death of the legendary broadcaster. Peel referred to Yorkston as 'the finest singer-songwriter of his generation'.

Yorkston lived in Fife until he left school, and later returned to the area to raise his family. He has carved out a niche career across a series of much admired and uncompromising albums between 2002 and now, including the excellent collaborative project Yorkston, Thorne, Khan. Prolific across different media, in more recent years he has turned his hand to writing tour diaries and has had two novels published.

On the west coast a new crop of young songwriters was emerging, with the charts in their sights. Inspired by seeing Travis at 'T in the Park', a teenage Amy Macdonald picked up a guitar and began writing. After sending off a demo, she was spotted and mentored by two established songwriters before signing a deal with Vertigo Records. Though softly spoken, her booming singing voice displayed the power of a young Grace Slick of Jefferson Airplane. With the added depth and

James Yorkston at the Greenman Festival, Glanusk Park, Brecon Beacons, Wales, 2008

shot2bits.net_westmacott / Alamy Stock Photo

Amy Macdonald at Scotland v Spain, UEFA European Championship qualifier, 12 October 2010

Allstar Picture Library / Alamy Stock Photo

maturity of songwriting, her debut album *This Is The Life* was released in 2007 and promptly shifted an amazing three million copies. It's fascinating that Macdonald has never relied on the fickle UK pop market, but established her career across Europe where she is well loved. To date, at only thirty, she has released four albums and continually scored chart-topping singles in Germany, Switzerland, Belgium, France and Spain. An inspiration to young women, her plain-speaking, acoustic songs and work ethic is a credit to the nation.

If the city of Paisley gave us Gerry Rafferty and helped champion punk in the 1970s, its biggest recent triumph has been local lad Paolo Nutini. Gifted with a husky, impassioned voice and chiselled, Italian cheekbones, he has it all – guys want to be him, girls want to be *with* him. This aside, Nutini has shown himself to be a singular artist over his career so far. Expected to follow his father into the fish'n'chip shop business, Paolo's talent was caught and signed at only eighteen. Initially seen by some of the public and media as a disposable-pop singer and a major label construct, he has since proved to be the exact opposite. With his eyes shut, jazz

Paolo Nutini, FIB Festival, Benicassim,
Spain, 20 July 2014

Christian Bertrand / Shutterstock.com

cigarette in hand, hunched-over stage persona and gravel-strewn tonsils, Nutini has more in common with American soul-singer Wilson Pickett, Jamaican reggae icon Toots Hibbert, or even a young Rod Stewart. The music may be soul-driven and familiar, but elements of his Paisley accent creep into the delivery too.

Over three albums – *These Streets*, *Sunny Side Up* and *Caustic Love* – he has blended soul, funk, reggae, jazz and psychedelia to create a sound all his own, without pandering to fads or fashion. One of the last signings made by Ahmet Ertegun to the Atlantic Label in 2005, Nutini played support to a re-formed Led Zeppelin at an Ertegun tribute concert in 2007 and has gone on to share stages effortlessly with acts such as The Rolling Stones and Amy Winehouse over the years. He also has a list of awards and nominations including a coveted Ivor Novello. Given his quality and idiosyncratic musical decisions, his popularity across Europe and increasingly in the States, he could be one of the greats in years to come.

As a reserved, down-to-earth guy, Paolo Nutini is a genuine star, with his sell-out Bellahouston Park concert in 2015, memorable 'T in the Park' sets and an Edinburgh's Hogmanay headline slot in the bag. Appealing to alternative and mainstream audiences alike, songs like *New Shoes*, *Candy*, *Pencil Full Of Lead* and *Iron Sky* are most definitely modern-day classics.

Indie bands and singer-songwriters may have been thick on the ground, but Scotland's 'heavy' scene needed a boost. Scotland had little homegrown hard rock to boast about since groups like Nazareth and The Sensational Alex Harvey Band, until a trio from Kilmarnock turned up – Biffy Clyro – though they were lost in the wilderness for almost a decade before connecting with the audience they deserved. Their early years from 1995 saw the band release a single on the label of their friends Aereogramme, and team up with Electric Honey Records for an EP before inking a deal with the independent Beggars Banquet in 2000. Never has a band worked so hard to make an impression as the twin Johnstone brothers (Ben on drums, James on bass), alongside best friend Simon Neil on guitar and vocals. Climbing into their transit van, they played every nook and cranny available across the UK, while releasing ambitious albums *Blackened Sky*, *The Vertigo Of Bliss* and *Infinity Land*. Taking the visceral attack of Nirvana, the melodic versatility of Far, and injecting some math rock into the mix, they developed a melodic form of heaviness that immediately had cross-over potential. Here was a band with a penchant for loud guitars and prison tattoos, with their hearts firmly fixed on the mainstream.

Most bands give up when their dreams don't swiftly come true. Biffy Clyro and their dedicated manager stuck at it, eventually penning a deal in 2006 with a Warner Brothers' offshoot, 14th Floor Recordings. With the deal in place and years of slog and experience behind them, they grasped the opportunity and upped their game. Fourth album *Puzzle* (2007) hit the number-two slot and suddenly the rock world wanted a piece of them. They would play with Queens of the Stone Age, Red Hot Chili Peppers and Bon Jovi among others, while building that all-important fan-base little by little. And so devoted are these fans that many now have Biffy tattoos and share the photos online. *Only Revolutions* (2009) contained the band's first top-ten single *Mountains*, which remains a fan favourite and cemented their reputation in the big league, enabling them to headline Knebworth's Sonisphere festival. But it would be the preposterous double album *Opposites* (2013) that would finally hit the number-two spot. After sell-out shows at Glasgow's SECC, The Hydro, 'TRNSMT' festival and their own Bellahouston Park gig, as well as headlining Reading, Leeds and 'Download' at Donnington Park, Biffy Clyro have written their own, remarkable rags-to-riches story and taken the nation with them. Not simply a rock band, their appeal welcomes mainstream fans and even saw X-Factor winner Matt Cardle cover one of their songs *Many Of Horror (When We Collide)* in 2010. With another album *Ellipsis* (2016) hitting number one, and with *NME*, *Q* and *Kerrang* awards under their belt and yet more global touring, they are now quite possibly the biggest rock band in the UK. 'Mon the Biffy!

As a consequence Scotland is now renowned as a rock breeding-ground, with Twin Atlantic quickly following in Biffy's footsteps. The Glasgow quartet originally formed in the early 2000s, but took a slow but steady route to find their feet through local gigs and self-funded releases. Playing riff-heavy, non-conformist math rock on their debut album *Vivarium* (2009), they quickly about-turned to write massive FM anthems on their second album *Free*, landing the band in the top forty. Since then they've continued that approach on two further albums, *The Great Divide* (2014) and

GLA (2016), breaking into the top ten on both occasions and winning over an ever-expanding army of teenage fans. With Sam McTrusty's Glasgow brogue distinctly heard on tracks such as *Heart & Soul* and *Brothers & Sisters*, the group has secured itself a place in Scottish hearts with sell-out shows at the Barrowland Ballroom and The Hydro, as well as a Radio 1 stage headline set at 'T in the Park' in 2015. Though not yet at the same level as their muses Biffy Clyro, they are a seriously successful act thanks to their hard gig schedule and flair for a catchy chorus. They have also paved the way for up-and-coming Scottish rockers such as Fatherson and Vukovi.

As the 2000s progressed, even indie music was splintering into different sub-genres. If Franz Ferdinand represented an artier aesthetic, then a more straight-talking, populist approach was also on hand. Post-Britpop, a certain demographic wanted loud guitars and sing-along choruses without the art-school excess and three new Scottish groups would fill the void perfectly. The Fratellis probably never have to work again after their ubiquitous *Chelsea Dagger* single with its knees-up 'na na na' chorus seemingly played at every sporting event. It was one of many outstanding songs on debut album *Costello Music* in 2006. This offering ram-raided its way into the public's consciousness due to the sheer catchiness of singles *Henrietta* and

Twin Atlantic at the Hurricane Festival, Scheesel, Germany, 24 June 2017

Sebastian Gollnow / dpa / Alamy Live News

Creepin' Up The Back Stairs. A trio from Glasgow, they appeared with fully-formed songs, cranked-up guitars, Ray Davies-esque social commentary and a wildman drummer called Mince. From the very start The Fratellis were a success and could have been even more popular as a classic British guitar group, had they not fallen out with each other and called it quits in 2009 after the second album *Here We Stand* (2008). Re-forming in 2012, however, they've won back their fans and continue to impress live and on recording. Singer Jon Lawler knows his way around a perfect pop song and has created a catalogue of lovable earworms across three more Fratellis albums, a solo collection and the side-project Codeine Velvet Club.

While The Fratellis were making waves, a gang from Dundee appeared on the scene. The View were in their late teens when their ramshackle post-Libertines racket was unearthed by local label Two Thumbs before being taken on by London's 1965 Recordings. In months they would go from local unknowns playing cover versions in the Bayview pub to nationwide stars, thanks to Radio 1's Zane Lowe and others. The Dryburgh quartet's debut album *Hats Off To The Buskers* (2007) became an indie-punk classic, reaching number one and earning a Mercury Music Prize nomination. The album recently celebrated its tenth anniversary, with ditties such as *Same Jeans*,

The Fratellis at the Macrobert Arts Centre,
Stirling, 2012

Wasted Little DJs and *Superstar Trades-man* still resonating on radio and at festivals. Undeniable childhood camaraderie and a reputation for wild partying aside, the band toured internationally and have played 'T in the Park' a record eight times. Since forming in 2005 they have exhibited an instinctive grasp of classic pop-writing with the soulful rasp of singer Kyle Falconer up front. Although their initial commercial promise was never quite achieved, they have released a series of four more impressive albums which, despite being unfairly ignored by critics, have showcased their love of soul, folk and rootsy rock'n'roll. The View's music has always remained powerful and hook-laden, and they continue to tour and release music to an adoring public, with Falconer about to unleash a solo album.

Glasvegas are another group who fleetingly stepped into the limelight and were heralded as the saviours of rock'n'roll, only to fade from sight at the very peak of their popularity. From Dalmarnock in the East of Glasgow, the band is a songwriting vehicle for former professional footballer James Allan. Their sound combines the effects-laden chime of U2 and the righteous fuzz of the Jesus and Mary Chain, set to a Phil Spector-esque 'wall of sound' production and a love of '60s classicism. Allan's acute and gritty storytelling sees the lyrics of *Daddy's Gone, It's My Own Cheating Heart That Makes Me Cry* and *Geraldine* deal with domestic violence, infidelity and social work, projected in his own Glasgow burr. It was no surprise that Creation mogul Alan McGee took to them immediately at a Glasgow gig. Building a following in London, the group would eventually sign to Sony/Columbia after a series of self-released singles and support from the *New Musical Express* media mafia of the time; while McGee's own hyperbole proclaimed them as the 'greatest band since the Mary Chain'. Launching in 2003, Glasvegas entered the public's consciousness as their self-titled debut album hit number two in 2008, winning a Mercury nomination like fellow Scots Primal Scream, Franz Ferdinand, KT Tunstall and The View before them.

Global touring, supports to Oasis, U2 and Kings of Leon, and unanimous critical approval helped to sell thousands of copies of the Glasvegas debut album before they retired to Santa Monica, California, to record the follow-up. With a head of steam and a worldwide fanbase waiting for another collection, their undoing was possibly the easy-going Californian way of life. After months of writing and recording, they

returned to the UK in 2011 with the oblique, unfocused *Euphoric /// Heartbreak * album. Alongside its confusing title and hazier sound, the group decided to abandon their trademark black leather and shades for an all-white image. It was brave, but the public didn't buy it. Despite the album going top ten, sales were disappointing and the band was dropped after its release. To their credit they didn't call it a day, but rallied to produce a third album in 2013 *Later ... When The TV Turns To Static*, with a new deal with BMG in place. This saw a return to their original sound and leather chic with another strong collection, though unfortunately it did not chart highly. Glasvegas have been responsible for some truly heroic pop over their career and a new set is rumoured to appear soon. A comeback is never out of the question.

Camera Obscura are a stealth indie band whose understated delivery and wistful song-craft has crept into the hearts of an adoring global audience. Beginning in 1996 as a vehicle for Traceyanne Campbell's songwriting, their debut album *Biggest Bluest Hi-Fi* set out their stall with production duties by Stuart Murdoch of Belle & Sebastian. Initially seen as the Belles' wee sister band, their own identity and melancholic, melodic flourishes developed over the course of five superb albums showcasing a real talent. Camera Obscura is the sound of '60s soul, '70s soft rock and crystallised

Glasvegas, Milano, Italy, 2009

MARKA / Alamy Stock Photo

'C86' indie pop colliding across lush instrumentation, with Campbell's maudlin vocal inflections instilling the songs with a sense of heartbreak. Now as popular Stateside as in Europe, the group is signed to the influential 4AD label which has helped their profile grow and made them more commercial. In 2015, however, long-time keyboard player and backing vocalist Carey Lander sadly died of osteosarcoma. Being an integral band member and close friend of Campbell's, the group understandably took an indefinite hiatus. Campbell has only just recently returned to the fray in the duo Traceyanne and Danny (Coughlan), with a beautiful set of collaborative songs.

Through gargantuan guitar sounds, melancholy lyrical content and that all-important Scottish accent, Chemikal Underground, specifically its biggest exports Mogwai and Arab Strap, would exercise huge influence on the next generation of indie bands. Three groups that doffed their caps in their general direction appeared in the late 2000s and all signed to Fatcat Recordings in Brighton. Youngest of the batch, We Were Promised Jetpacks, are four schoolmates who formed a tight, dynamic rock band, embarking on a career over three albums to date. Singer-songwriter Adam Thompson's Edinburgh accent is easily detected within his anguished holler above the group's angular guitar, bass and drums attack. Their opening album *These Four Walls* (2009) immediately captured the imaginations of post-emo listeners who wanted something honest, passionate and direct. These days The Jetpacks create a powerful, modern Scottish rock music, both mysterious and straight-talking.

With guitarist Andy Macfarlane blending the sonic extremities of My Bloody Valentine and Mogwai with singer James Graham's disturbing lyrical imagery and affecting Kilsyth roar, The Twilight Sad has grown steadily from post-punk outsiders to a band capable of selling out the Barrowland Ballroom with a monumental and eardrum-shattering live show. Over four excellent albums they have set out their noisy 'shoegaze' and poetry template, where lilting folk melodies and unusual wordplay hit screaming guitars head on. Their debut *Fourteen Autumns And Fifteen Winters* (2007) immediately appealed to the embryonic indie blogosphere and its network of promoters, helping them to tour globally and publicise the album and its follow-up, *Forget the Night Ahead* (2009). With a line-up change and slight career wobble on their more industrial, electronic third album *No One Can Ever Know* (2012), they regained lost ground on the superb return to form *Nobody Wants To Be Here And Nobody Wants To Leave* (2014), and a tour of the USA and Europe as support to The Cure. Although the band has since been quiet, with Graham working on a side project Out Lines with 'Scottish Album of the Year' award-winner Kathryn Joseph, the group promise a return in 2018. With their blistering catalogue and expanding audience, they too will prove to be an important Scottish group.

Most successful of these three is Frightened Rabbit – the *nom-de-plume* of Selkirk songwriter Scott Hutchison and a nickname given to him by his mother. Since 2003 his visceral, emotive outbursts on love, sex, religion and mortality have seen his band grow from a duo with his brother Grant, to a trio, and to a fully-fledged quintet featuring Billy Kennedy, Andy Monaghan and Simon Liddell. They have headlined huge venues and festival stages at home and abroad, especially across the USA. Fresh out of art school, the first album *Sing The Greys* (2006) on the Hits the Fan label was largely Scott and Grant's work with a mix of skewed folk and indie rock under-pinning Hutchison's Borders-accented yelp. Grabbing Fatcat Recordings' attention they let loose their best-loved album, *The Midnight Organ Fight* (2008), a break-up scrapbook of such raw and intense proportions that it inspired utter devotion in all who discovered it. *The Modern Leper* and *Keep Yourself Warm* are huge crowd sing-alongs to this day, and the band recently played the entire album live to celebrate its tenth anniversary. With occasional songs synchronised on US television dramas such as 'Grey's Anatomy', the group's popularity rose sharply across the pond and allowed them to tour the continent to an expectant audience before they had one in the UK.

Third album *The Winter of Mixed Drinks* (2010) affirmed their gradual ascent, showing a more textured and expansive sound across standout singles *Swim Until You Can't See Land* and *Living In Colour*. With a growing fanbase and three critically-acclaimed records in the bag, Atlantic Records stepped in and helped turn them into a powerful rock act with *Pedestrian Verse* (2013) and *Painting Of A Panic Attack* (2016).

Scott Hutchison was one of the hardest-working, most prolific performers on the underground circuit, and regularly played at charity and friends' events. He released a solo album as Owl John and recently made a noisy rock album with his brother and another set of brothers, James and Justin Lockey, under the name

Mastersystem. Despite or perhaps because of his personal traumas, the group's appeal always lay in Scott's heart-on-sleeve, confessional writing on his struggles with mental health, depression and various doomed relationships. In May 2018, however, the Frightened Rabbit story wretchedly came to an end. To a monumental outpouring of grief from across Scotland and the world, the shock announcement came that Scott Hutchison had disappeared and was then found dead, having taken his own life. It is nothing short of a tragedy.

Scotland has seen a real upsurge in its electronic music scene in the last decade or so. Some of its blossoming artists have become far more successful than most rock bands. At the start of the 2000s perhaps the most important breakthrough artist was Isle of Skye musician Myles MacInnes, aka Mylo. His funky, filtered-house productions injected fun and sheer pop into the mix and saw his only album *Destroy Rock'n'Roll* become a global hit, with singles *In My Arms*, *Drop the Pressure*, *Muscle Car* and mash-up *Doctor Pressure* all created on a computer in his bedroom. Though hugely successful from 2004–7, Mylo has remained relatively quiet since and there's no sign of a follow-up. We live in hope.

Frightened Rabbit at the Latitude Festival, Suffolk, 2010

Photograph by Nick Pickles
WENN Ltd / Alamy Stock Photo

Though largely anonymous, collectives such as NMBRS and LuckyMe have appeared in Edinburgh and Glasgow to promote club-nights, digital releases, fashion, design and parties. DJs and producers like Jackmaster, Éclair Fifi, Rustie and Hudson Mohawke (Ross Birchard a.k.a. Hudmo) have blended hip hop, house, techno, dubstep, rhythm'n'blues and '80s synths to create forms that push pop into the future. LuckyMe has seen Rustie and Hudson Mohawke sign to electronica epicentre Warp Records, with label boss Dominic Flanagan now A&R manager. Hudmo is the most renowned, having gone from teenage hip-hop fanatic and DMC turntablist to world-class DJ, artist and remixer. His albums *Butter* (2009) and *Lantern* (2015) have seen him reinvent production technique, with EPs such as *Satin Panthers* breaking new ground. He also collaborates with Canadian producer Lunice as TNGHT, and has produced tracks for Antony Hegarty as Anohni. Perhaps his most high profile work has been making beats for Kanye West, A$AP Rocky and Drake via West's G.O.O.D. Music label, with production on *Yeezus* (2013) and *The Life Of Pablo* (2016).

Perhaps Scotland's most influential and lauded electronic group is also its most secretive. Balerno brothers Michael Sandison and Marcus Eoin became known as Boards of Canada in the mid-'90s and attracted global recognition after the release of their debut album *Music Has The Right To Children* (1998) on electronica powerhouse, Warp Records. Swept in alongside new producers such as Aphex Twin, Autechre and LFO, their individual style was defined by a collage of hazy melodies, wonky analogue synths, hip-hop breakbeats, sampled voices and found-sounds. They have since created a series of sacred, psychedelic dreamscapes over four full-length albums and EPs, garnering a fanatical cult following. Theirs is an idiosyncratic world that shares a sense of nostalgia but also futurism, combining themes of nature, numerology and the supernatural. Having not played a live show – nor appeared in public to anyone's knowledge – since 2001, their elusive and enigmatic persona has increased their popularity, with last album *Tomorrow's Harvest* hitting number seven in the UK charts in 2013. More recently making use of the internet as a tool for connecting directly with their followers, the duo has somehow retained their air of mystery while crafting revered electronic music for the world.

The electronic group Chvrches has its roots in the indie underground. With Iain

Cook in Aereogramme and The Unwinding Hours, Martin Doherty moonlighting with The Twilight Sad and singer Lauren Mayberry part of Blue Sky Archives, they put their extensive experience into a synth-pop melting-pot and produced a batch of killer songs in their Glasgow studio. Under a search-engine-friendly name, first track *Lies* was unearthed through the 'Neon Gold' blog, and live shows were played under a pseudonym. Using the internet to create a buzz around a new act, they drip-fed a hyped-up audience track-by-track to build up anticipation until they could let loose their debut album *The Bones Of What You Believe*. The result took the band straight across the world, with top-ten hits in many charts. Sonically and strategically they are a phenomenon of the twenty-first century. On their second outing *Every Eye Open*, they updated their '80s-influenced sound, fostering a global, digital community of fans. New album *Love is Dead* (2018) further reveals Mayberry's bittersweet lyrical obsessions over crystalline synth lines and sugar-coated melodies. Without anyone really noticing, Chvrches are now one of the biggest pop acts on Earth.

Who would have imagined twenty-year-old Adam Wiles becoming a global megastar when stacking shelves in a Dumfries retailer, but he now strides like a hit-making colossus over the pop world under alter-ego Calvin Harris. Discovered via the Myspace social network, he signed to Sony Records and EMI Music Publishing with the help of DJ and mentor Mike Pickering of M People. Debut album *I Created Disco* (2007) may have been a cheeky punk-funk foot in the charts, but since album *Ready For The Weekend* (2009) and even more successful sequel *18 Months* (2012), his career has gone through the roof. Collaborations with Rihanna, Kelis, Dizzee Rascal, Tinchy Stryder, Ne-Yo, Florence Welsh, Frank Ocean, Pharrell Williams and others, are all at the peak of the entertainment game. His omnipresent electronic dance music and electro-house anthems are addictive and never far from the top of the charts; while his private life and relationships with Rita Ora and Taylor Swift have been splattered across every gossip column. Harris has performed DJ residencies in Las Vegas and regularly tops the Forbes List of multi-millionaire musicians. *Motion* (2014) and *Funk Wav Bounces Vol. 1* (2017) albums have bolstered his reputation and wealth, making him the most successful male solo artist in the USA since Michael Jackson. Not bad for a guy who began at fifteen creating dance music in his Dumfries bedroom.

Black American music has played a big part in Scottish pop from the 1950s onwards. As Scotland has become more multi-cultural, its ethnic make-up and music has also evolved. Aberdonian Emeli Sandé is testament to that, with an English mother and Zambian father. In her relatively short career to date she has clocked up two chart-topping albums in *Our Version Of Events* and *Long Live The Angels*, both showcasing her polished but earnest rhythm'n'blues, soul and pop. She has also won two Brit Awards, performed at the London Olympics ceremonies and been given an MBE for services to music. Sande is genuine knockout success and a veritable, modern pop star with massive mainstream appeal.

As hip hop took hold in the latter part of the twentieth century, Scotland would also take it to its heart. Though the country is not as ethnically diverse as other parts of the UK, the power and precision of rap has certainly made its impact here. As producers such as Hudmo moved into the light, rappers and vocalists have likewise raised their profile. In recent years the Glasgow rapper and social justice campaigner Loki has been an uncompromising and outspoken voice in the media, Edinburgh collective Stanley Odd has released five albums through various labels and toured the UK, while Paisley-born bad-boy Shogun is a hero of home-grown grime. The group gaining plaudits on a worldwide stage, however, is Young Fathers.

Alloysious Massaquoi, Kayus Bankole and Graham 'G' Hastings are a multi-ethnic Edinburgh trio with heritage from Liberia and Nigeria as well as Scotland. Joining forces at an underage hip-hop club in the early 2000s their initial musical exploits were under the name 3-Style, making rap-infused pop. With the help of local management they became Young Fathers in 2008, progressing into vibrant, vaguely psychedelic territory inhabited by the likes of Outkast and the Beastie Boys. Grabbing the industry's attention they would soon have an altercation with their management and disappear underground. Re-emerging under producer Tim London, with a darker, more ominous sound of soul, dub, post-punk and industrial textures, they were randomly signed by the alternative American hip-hop stable Anticon in 2012 to release new material as *Tape One* and *Tape Two* mini-albums. The second set went on to win the 2013 'Scottish Album of the Year', while third album *Dead*, their most direct mission statement yet, came through a new label Big Dada and won the

Mercury Music Prize, establishing them as one of the UK's most cutting-edge acts.

The prolific trio went on to make the *White Men Are Black Men Too* album in 2015, to yet more recognition. They released a collaborative EP with trip-hop legends Massive Attack when the band shared stages on tour. Being based in Leith also had its advantages, with Irvine Welsh and Danny Boyle featuring a five Young Fathers' numbers in the 'T2–Trainspotting' film soundtrack. Their newest collection *Cocoa Sugar* has just been issued and garnered their best reviews and radio-play to date; and with praise rightfully raining down on the band from all corners they play sell-out shows and festival headline sets. Young Fathers represent a new, diverse, multi-cultural Scotland that is forward-thinking and progressive. Watch them claim the future.

Scotland in 2018 has a varied spread of world-beaters and underground icons across genres and styles, all propelling the world of rock and pop into new stylistic areas. Its history and heritage are exceptional, with catalogues of timeless music for all to investigate on disc and online. As you read this book the next chapter is already writing itself as the stars of the future hone their skills and ready themselves for the next pop takeover. Perhaps, for Scotland, this is only the beginning.

Young Fathers at Liverpool Sound City Festival, England 2016

Michelle Roberts / Alamy Stock Photo

Chapter ten
Throw the 'R' away

What does it mean to be Scottish? Can we celebrate Scottish-ness? And if so, how do we do it? Such questions are not easily answered. Every country's identity is made up of countless ethnicities and attitudes; and homogenisation does not sit well in Scotland. There are notable cultural differences between east and west, Highland and Lowland, metropolitan and rural, Catholic and Protestant, middle class and working class – but is there something that binds us all together?

For tourists and travellers, the nation is often defined by words such as 'Braveheart', 'whisky' or 'kilts' – but since the dawn of pop culture as we know it, a slow

but steady transition has been taking place as the country morphs into a vibrant, modern, outward-facing country.

There is a definite aesthetic heritage, thanks to our fabrics, our cultural tropes and diverse countryside. Tartan, whisky and stunning landscapes remain a major draw for visitors, and no matter where you travel here, you'll find a warm welcome, a decent bite to eat and a unique souvenir or two to purchase amid geographic splendour. At the same time, independent businesses and tourism initiatives have helped the textile and craft industries to experience a renaissance, while Scottish food and drink products are marketed worldwide to great acclaim.

As we celebrate 'The History of Scottish Pop' in this book, it is perhaps relevant to ask what actually makes a musician Scottish? Do we count the Young brothers of AC/DC, Mark

Pages 182–83: A jacket worn by a
member of the Bay City Rollers

On loan from a Private Collection
Image © National Museums Scotland

Rod Stewart, early 1970s

Courtesy of CSU Archives / Everett
Collection Historical / Alamy Stock Photo

Knopfler of Dire Straits or David Byrne from Talking Heads because they were born in Glasgow and Dumbarton? Country and western star Johnny Cash can claim family roots in Dunfermline, while gravel-voiced Rod Stewart, though not born in Scotland, famously supports Celtic Football Club and dons a tartan scarf at any opportunity, proudly declaring his Scottish ancestry. Tartan itself is emotive and can trigger different reactions. Many simply see the shortbread tin of yesteryear, while others revel in it. Attend a wedding, graduation or rugby match in Scotland these days and you will witness more kilts worn than ever before. Some musicians, like the Bay City Rollers, used tartan in a slightly gimmicky way – on trousers, shirts and scarves – but The Rollers in their hey-day were celebrated just as much at home as anywhere else.

Vivienne Westwood and Malcolm McLaren may have displayed an obsession with tartan during punk, but others used it in a more tongue-in-cheek way. Contentiously proclaiming themselves 'The Sound of Young Scotland' in 1980, Postcard Records occasionally adorned record sleeves with kilted highlanders during the post-punk era, alongside their logo of a grinning kitten beating a drum. Arab Strap once wore full Highland dress for promotional photos, simultaneously showing their pride in being Scottish while sending the whole thing up. Some are po-faced and partisan about it, others have a more self-effacing and lighthearted approach. Let's not forget surrealist poet, songwriter and humourist Ivor Cutler – a Scot to his core, but never afraid of taking a bizarre, sideways look at his roots, culture and upbringing across many albums and broadcasts. And no book on Scottish pop would be complete without a mention of the inimitable Jesse Rae. A true eccentric from St Boswells in the Scottish Borders, many will know his arresting aesthetic of kilt, helmet, armour and wielded claymore but see it as comedic and throwaway. However, with links to serious musicians from Parliament and Funkadelic, as well as UK reggae stable On-U Sound, his reputation is cemented across a series of truly funky singles and albums from the late 1970s until today. And there is also 'Tartan Week' in the USA, with a series of parades across central New York City. As the event develops, it is taking on a more contemporary feel with modern music alongside the bagpipes.

It is increasingly obvious that music of all kinds has been encouraged within communities across Scotland for centuries. But as in the UK as a whole, and recently

in Europe, the ever-present trans-Atlantic drawl has been the mainstay vocal delivery of pop songs since the 1950s. But these days the colloquial influence of Scots and Gaelic languages can be heard once again in pop culture. As in literature, theatre, television and film, music forges ever forward and assists the rediscovery of native accents and words. Though you might hear a tinge of accent from Alex Harvey or Jack Bruce in the '60s and '70s, it was not until the '80s that the idea would start to become normalised in contemporary Scottish pop. Enter The Proclaimers and their self-assured Auchtermuchty pronunciation as they threw the 'R' away.

Outwith folk and traditional musicians, who have always used their own accent, many current artists do this too and find success far beyond Scotland. Arab Strap's influence has been huge, an acclaimed, underground indie act trying not to sound American or from London but singing in their mother tongue. Another influential voice is King Creosote, who has employed a natural burr within his songs from the '90s to the present day. Now Biffy Clyro, The Twilight Sad, Frightened Rabbit, Glasvegas, Twin Atlantic and even Paolo Nutini can be heard flaunting their own accent.

KT Tunstall at the Tartan Day Parade,
New York City, USA, 7 April 2018

Geisler-Fotopress / Alamy Stock Photo

And as hip hop makes its mark, Scottish rappers mine the poetry of local streets and housing schemes. Listen to Loki, Shogun, Solareye, Freestyle Master and Respek BA – the country they hail from is obvious.

Throughout the twentieth century and beyond, there has been something of a cultural cringe regarding some of Scotland's heritage, culture and language. This is now on the wane, due in part to the international success and confidence of its musicians, actors and artists, but also thanks to a recent galvanising movement in modern Scottish politics. The two are not mutually exclusive. As confidence in the nation has grown, so has its different voices. Scottish nationalism was only the concern of a small part of society until the turn of the decade, never amounting to more than approximately twenty per cent of the vote. By the time of the recent Independence Referendum in 2014 this had grown to forty-five per cent, with the rise of so-called 'civic nationalism'. The 'Yes' and 'No' campaigns made effective use of social media and young people especially seemed politically engaged for the first time in a generation – on both sides of the argument.

Above and beyond an international love of ceilidh music and Scottish country dancing, Scotland can now declare itself a music tourism destination. Glasgow in particular has city music tours, an infrastructure of clubs, live venues, recording studios, rehearsal spaces and array of fledgling labels. Holidaymakers come to the city to enjoy the nightlife and creativity, and an increasing number of young people move here to study for the same reason. The 'Scottish Album of the Year' award has been running since 2012, with winners including Bill Wells and Aidan Moffat, RM Hubbert, Young Fathers, Kathryn Joseph, Anna Meredith and Sacred Paws. On a par with the Mercury Music Prize, it is the biggest arts award in the country. The 'Tartan Clef Awards' have been rebranded the 'Scottish Music Awards' with all proceeds donated to the Nordoff Robbins music charity. There are even the youthful and enthusiastic 'Scottish Alternative Music Awards', developed from a college project in Glasgow.

The arts-funding organisation Creative Scotland has also provided a lifeline to many artists, enabling them to tour, record and release music in an age when the industry surrounding it has taken a beating. With internet streaming and downloading affecting traditional sales, alternative models have had to be considered. With a smaller, streamlined, DIY industry taking hold, music conferences like 'Xpo-North' and 'Wide Days' have sprung up to help local artists take their destiny into their own hands.

Listening to seven decades of music across multiple genres, has Scottish pop developed any kind of particular sound? We have discussed its affinity with Black American music, and there are the indigenous Celtic melodies. But perhaps rather than a sound, there is a collective attitude. One that comes from a sense of outsider struggle, hardship, being ignored or sidelined. A feeling of melancholy and hopelessness, juxtaposed with some kind of joy or euphoria. Maybe triumph over adversity.

At any rate, with such cold, rainy, dreich weather in this country, it is necessary to make your own fun indoors – hence the appeal of telling stories and singing songs around a roaring fire in a pub or club. Music is definitely in the blood here, but being at a distance from London has perhaps enabled Scottish acts to develop their own idiosyncratic vision. The Scots possess a unique stubbornness and dogged determination and that manifests itself in its art.

To those willing to investigate, Scotland now has a less parochial, more enlightened music scene than ever, and it stands alongside the rest of the world in the digital age. Artists such as Young Fathers, Calvin Harris and Chvrches now perform on a global stage and many fans don't even know where their favourites are from. Does that make these artists, or their music, any less Scottish? Of course not. Thankfully, Scotland is more comfortable than ever honouring its own folk culture and traditional roots, while stretching beyond that to incorporate outside elements and to be more international in outlook and appeal. With an impressive musical legacy behind it, this new, confident, progressive Scotland is now capable of celebrating its past, its present and its future.

Opposite: The Proclaimers, 1991

Photo by Murdo Macleod

Index of bands and artists